*The*
# Colorless Womb

# *The* Colorless Womb

*Kimberly Gowdy*

Alpharetta, GA

Some names and identifying details have been changed to protect the privacy of individuals.

The author has tried to recreate events, locations, and conversations from her memories of them. In some instances, in order to maintain their anonymity, the author has changed the names of individuals and places. She may also have changed some identifying characteristics and details such as physical attributes, occupations, and places of residence.

Copyright © 2021 Kimberly Gowdy

All rights reserved. No part of this book may be reproduced or transmitted in any form or by any means, electronic or mechanical, including photocopying, recording, or any information storage and retrieval system, without permission in writing from the publisher. For more information, address BookLogix, c/o Permissions Department, 1264 Old Alpharetta Rd., Alpharetta, GA 30005.

ISBN: 978-1-63183-791-3 - Paperback
eISBN: 978-1-63183-792-0 - ePub
eISBN: 978-1-63183-793-7 - mobi

Library of Congress Control Number: 2020919111

Printed in the United States of America            0 1 0 4 2 1

☉ This paper meets the requirements of ANSI/NISO Z39.48-1992 (Permanence of Paper)

*I dedicate this book to my husband, Dave, and my son, Doc, your love made this book possible. You are God's greatest gifts to me, and He has given me many. Because of your love, I was able to fulfill a dream. I also dedicate this book to M.O.B.Y. (Mommy Older Baby Younger), my fellow Intended Parents, and to anyone who's ever had to endure the pain of infertility. It's never too late to follow your dreams.*

*May God bless you as He has blessed me.*

*In Memoriam*
*Elijah Brandon Garrett*
*You will never be forgotten.*


*For everything there is a season,*
*and a time for every matter under heaven.*

—Ecclesiastes 3:1

# Contents

*Foreword*   ix
*Preface*   xi

**Prologue**   1
**Chapter 1:** The Big One   5
**Chapter 2:** Letting Go   11
**Chapter 3:** It Happened Again   15
**Chapter 4:** What's Up, Doc?   21
**Chapter 5:** Welcome to Atlanta   29
**Chapter 6:** Home Sweet Home   35
**Chapter 7:** I Do   39
**Chapter 8:** Elijah   47
**Chapter 9:** Roller Coaster   55
**Chapter 10:** What We Do for Love   59
**Chapter 11:** The Decision   63
**Chapter 12:** Strike 1, 2, 3!   69
**Chapter 13:** Not Again   81
**Chapter 14:** Off to a Good Start   87
**Chapter 15:** She Said?   93
**Chapter 16:** So Far, So Good   97
**Chapter 17:** Keeping Busy   101
**Chapter 18:** Is She?   107
**Chapter 19:** Civic Duty   111
**Chapter 20:** I've Got News for You   115
**Chapter 21:** The Transition   121

**Chapter 22:** Feeling Guilty 125
**Chapter 23:** Tell Us How You *Really* Feel 129
**Chapter 24:** It's a Boy . . . It's a Girl 133
**Chapter 25:** Here Comes the Judge 139
**Chapter 26:** Let's Set a Date 145
**Chapter 27:** Don't Shut Me Out 149
**Chapter 28:** Final Touches 153
**Chapter 29:** We Have Your Back 155
**Chapter 30:** This Is the Day 161
**Chapter 31:** This Moment 167
**Chapter 32:** The Adjustment 179
**Chapter 33:** Move-in Day 183
**Chapter 34:** Shower Me with Your Love 187
**Chapter 35:** New York, New York 195
**Chapter 36:** Nothing Compares to You 199
**Epilogue** 201

# Foreword

*What color is the baby?*

There's no such thing as a bad question, only juvenile ones. Thank God I only thought it until now. That question was the first thing that popped in my mind when Kimberly, an African American woman, told me the birth mother of her child was Caucasian.

Her story is honest and transparent to the point that you actually experience her pain and cheer her successes. Kim Gowdy removes the mask from the struggle of not physically being able to carry and give birth, to reveal the joy of finally having a child to call her own.

If you've lived anytime on this planet, you know in life, situations can become hard to bear and you feel like giving up, caving in, and quitting. *The Colorless Womb* is an inspirational journey on how to stay the course, never give up on your heart's desire, and learn that second chances are possible—if you believe.

Whether you are a child, a husband, or someone escaping a bad relationship or starting a new career, this book will fuel you to achieve your goals.

—Tammy Dele
Founder and producer of Tammy'Dele Films

# Preface

As a child, I watched my dad and mom work hard, raise a family, and arm us with values that would take us through life. Being the oldest of six children I had the privilege of welcoming each new addition to our family. My dad always received the news over the phone. Back then the father wasn't so up close and personal during the delivery, if you know what I mean. "It's a girl," I could hear the nurse say. The scowl on my dad's face after hearing this for the fourth time was priceless. No doubt by then, he was hoping for a boy. It seemed as if my mom was back on her feet in no time. The beauty of birthing a baby, such a natural process, my mom made it look easy. So the saying goes, like mother like daughter. Although I bear a strong resemblance to my mother on the outside, on the inside we couldn't be more different. I knew I desired to experience the joy of motherhood and always believed I would, just not as many experiences as my mom.

But what happens when there is a disconnect between your desire and your reality? When your heart says yes but your body says no?

For the past four years I have wanted to "give birth" to a thing, and this book has allowed me that opportunity. This writing is intended for anyone with a dream, a goal, or a vision. I believe that through sharing my personal experience of the heartache, pain, and anguish that accompany any setback, as well as the relief, joy, and the victory of a dream realized, I can bless someone else. Through my journey I learned the gift of life is beautiful, and someone willing to "gift" you life is just as beautiful.

Many questioned my decision, some simply didn't understand, while others rejoiced and applauded my success. But to all who accompanied me on this journey, I say thank you.

I could not have made it to this place without the love of family and the grace of God. I believe that we are blessed to be a blessing.

# PROLOGUE

"I'm barren."

There, I said it. For years I could not and would not dare to openly admit to such a defect, the brokenness, and a sense of failure. I kept these feelings tucked away. After getting married, when asked about my desire to have children, I deflected to my go-to line, "I'm just not ready." Sure, I read about Sarah, Hannah, and Rachel in the Bible, but to say that I was a part of such a sorority was unthinkable.

A positive early pregnancy test followed by no heartbeat—that was often my narrative. It was easy to keep those losses a secret. With a little lipstick, eyedrops, and a fake smile, you can hide anything. But my nonchalant attitude toward starting a family became more difficult to hide. I was *showing*.

In fact, I was halfway down the field carrying the ball toward the end zone with the crowd cheering me on, but an unforeseen problem knocked me down, and I lost the ball. The loss was nothing like I'd ever imagined. The pain cut deep, and prayer became imperative. But I got back up, only to fumble the ball again.

My secret was out. It was suddenly obvious that it wasn't that I did not want, but that I could not have . . . A BABY.

So, it was time to be cut from the team—in this case, my marriage. What else could I do at this point except learn to be content with my current state? I could learn to accept that the one thing that I wanted more than anything was not within my reach. But didn't I read that God would give me the desires of my heart? Well, this was a desire. I desired to fill these empty arms.

I made plans for the second act of my life, but our plans are not always God's. A new love and a new hope came into my life. Suddenly, I knew I wasn't ready to give up! At this stage in my life, I realized I was much stronger than I'd given myself credit for. But what to do now?

Out of nowhere, the answer fell upon me, but it was up to me to be open to the unconventional.

Surrogacy? In my mind, this was only for the rich and famous, and I was neither. In the Bible, Sarah tried this with Hagar, and we know how that turned out. How badly did I desire a child? Did my desire for a child outweigh my pride? Was my desire bad enough to sign on the dotted line and trust my precious embryos to take hold within the womb of someone who wasn't me?

Yes, it was, and just like that, I started the journey. I needed to find a strong woman who could bear my infirmity. On our first attempt at surrogacy, I wasn't prepared to hear those familiar words, "I'm so sorry." We thought the second attempt and the second surrogate would be the ticket, but in the end, the pain was even more intense, as we had invested so much more time and energy. So, we moved on to who we believed would be our best and final surrogate. Strike three!

We are all taught the five stages of grief. I had finally moved into acceptance. Accepting that although I had stepped out on faith, my desire for a child would not come to fruition, my desire to fill the emptiness of my arms was not meant to be, and somehow I'd missed the mark and God had something else for me. When I had all but given up on my quest to become a mom, something unexpected happened. I received a phone call that changed my life, an offer from someone who I would never have sought out or looked to as a vessel to complete my journey, but she had stepped up to the plate.

Previously, I looked only to women who were black like me to fulfill my journey. Although they would share no biology with my child, I believed that I could see myself vicariously through them. I thought that our "sistah" bond would bring a sense of familiarity to our journey. But the last woman standing in my quest to become a mom didn't think like me, didn't live like me, and certainly didn't look like me. I'm black, she's white, and her name was Heidi, a name that is about as white as the name Shaquitta is black. Where I was broken, she was not. Where I delivered loss, she joyfully delivered the fruit of the womb.

I know blessings can come in unexpected forms. I believe it's God's way of showing us He's in charge. But I hadn't prepared for this. But even with all of our differences, she was open to the possibility. At the end of the day, I would have to decide if my desire to become a mom would be a hope deferred, or if I would ultimately join forces with a woman who could fulfill the desire of my heart.

The purpose of this book is not only to speak to women who are battling infertility, but also to anyone who needs reminding that our bodies are merely shells. Who we are and what we are run much deeper than skin color. With race relations at an all-time low, partly due to a broken political system, but mostly due to ignorance, I want you to walk away with a smile, a newfound joy, and a deeper awareness that we are more alike than we are different.

# CHAPTER 1

# THE BIG ONE

I was ready for this trip—like Calgon, take me away. I deserved this. We deserved this, my hubby and me. David and I have been married for six years. It was a second marriage for both of us. We needed time to relax and exhale. Our expectations were high, and we were giddy. Who knew that my husband, the overly serious Yale-educated doctor, could be giddy? The past five years had taken us on a journey of a lifetime mentally, physically, and financially.

So, in honor of yours truly, we were stepping out of Atlanta and heading to a celebration in New York City. This birthday was a milestone—not everyone could celebrate the big one in such style. I'm originally from Connecticut and David is from New Jersey, so celebrating in NYC made perfect sense. Having our guests come to Atlanta would have been a great idea, but we needed to get away, and for this kind of celebration a trip to Buckhead wouldn't do.

So, in August on New York City's East Side on a fabulous yacht and dressed in all white, friends and family would come to help me celebrate my fiftieth birthday. My actual birth date was a couple of months prior, but we wanted to pick a time that worked for most of our guests.

"Hun, do you think I should take these sandals?" I asked.

David rolled his eyes as only he could. "How many pairs of the same shoe can you pack?"

I side-eyed David as he walked away and thought to myself,

*Men will never understand that women need shoes like we need water.*

"I think I have everything," I said. I knew, in the back of my mind, I was sure to leave something behind.

"Remember, no more than two ounces of liquid in your carry-on," David yelled from the bedroom closet. I remembered to put socks in my purse since putting my bare feet on the airport floor gave me the creeps. I had already rummaged through my purse to make sure there were no sharp items in my carry-on. The last time TSA scanned me up and down, they took my tweezers. How do you deprive someone of a good brow?

By the time I got out of my thoughts, David had already made his way downstairs and was ready to load the bags in the car. He wanted to get us ahead of the morning rush hour. Atlanta has many great qualities, but the traffic isn't one of them. We were leaving for three days, but based on the amount of luggage, it looked like a month.

Typically, when David asked me what I wanted for my birthday I'd say, "Nothing." But this time when he asked, I quickly replied, "An all-white yacht party in New York City." Talk about being specific. With the help of my siblings and cousin Rachael, who was an NYC social butterfly, I knew it would be spectacular.

Before we left, I had to make my way to my son's room. We'd just changed his crib into a toddler bed. Where did the time go? As I stood in his room, running my fingers over his dresser, rubbing my hand over his stuffed animals, and looking at our family pictures, I could hardly believe how much my life had changed.

"You seem to be deep in thought," David said as he snuck up on me.

"Just thinking about life, things, and how I got to this place."

"Got to Atlanta?"

"Nooooo," I said playfully. "Just thinking back to how my life has changed." I was nostalgic.

"Of course your life has changed. You only met the man of your dreams," he joked.

"Whatever," I quipped. "The first time you saw me, I know you must have said, 'Lord, thank you for blessing me with her presence.'"

"I don't think so." David laughed and shook his head. The truth is, we were both right. "Okay, no more time for a trip down memory lane." David was ready to go.

Making our way down Georgia 400 is always a challenge. Regardless of what time you leave, the traffic will always let you know you should have left earlier. Because of that, we left extra early.

"Hun, make sure you have your ID, and remember, no sharp objects in the carry-ons," David rattled on. He couldn't help himself, but that's what I love about him. He always makes me feel loved.

"Did you take the perfume bottles out of the carry-on?" he continued.

"Yes, David, and I also remembered to put on my pants," I joked. We both laughed. David whipped the car down the highway. If we could get past Exit 7 without incident, we were home free. Exit 9 was looking fine. Exit 8 was looking great. Then, as if on cue, the brake lights lit up like a sea of Christmas lights. We'd built in a lot of additional time, but this highway was extremely unpredictable. Twenty minutes and five prayers later, we were back on track. Traffic had opened up right after Abernathy, and the rest was smooth sailing.

"Do you think it's too early to call?" I asked David. He looked over at the clock.

"Maybe not. Miss Loretta knows we're getting on the plane this morning, so she'll understand."

I made the call wirelessly. "Good morning," I heard a lovely voice say.

"Good morning, Miss Loretta. How are you?" Miss Loretta had been a Godsend. We met her through one of the nurses at the hospital where David worked. We interviewed several nannies, but the person who watched our little cherub had to meet our high comfort level and make us feel that he would be cared for, protected, and loved.

Miss Loretta certainly fit the bill. She had the sweetest spirit, was very soft-spoken, and had skin as smooth as a baby's bottom. She knew how to handle a baby, as she'd cared for her now grown children and had been a nanny for others. The moment she walked into our home, our spirits connected. So, after fifty questions, fingerprints, FBI background check, cameras installed in every room, and a drug test, I knew she was perfect.

Of course, I didn't require that level of security. Discernment was the biggest tool in my arsenal. What helped us make our final decision was easy. I went to the nursery, retrieved my baby, brought him downstairs, and placed him into her arms. Babies can sense love, and he melted right into her large bosom, the one that I don't have, and she cuddled my baby like he was her own. She held him like Big Mama, a term of endearment used for the matriarch in the African American community.

"I'm doing well," Miss Loretta said, "but I know you didn't call to find out how I'm doing." She was on to me.

I chuckled. "So, how is he?" I was beaming.

"Oh, dear, he's doing fine," she said. "He's right here. I'll let you talk to him." The next voice was one that meant everything. It was the voice I needed to hear.

"Mama," a wee voice called.

"Hi, baby. Whatcha doin'?" I said in an exaggerated voice.

I could hear Miss Loretta, helping him to answer me. "Tell Mommy that we're having breakfast," she whispered.

"Bradfast," he chimed. His voice was so sweet that I got chills every time I heard it.

"Mommy loves you, baby." I beamed.

"Hi, Doc," David joined in.

"Tell Mommy and Daddy you love them," I could hear a slightly muffled voice say. I knew that at only age two and a half and with *Sesame Street* in the background, talking to me didn't take priority, but I tried.

"Miss Loretta, please give him a kiss from Daddy and me," I said.

"I will," she responded.

"Okay, bye," I said, but I knew I'd call back later.

"Bye-bye," she replied in a soft voice.

David and I were already TSA cleared, so we got through check-in pretty quickly. Once we boarded, I was ready to relax. I knew hitting the streets of New York took energy. I needed to rest up now. I sat in the window seat. David always liked to sit on the outside. I was hoping I wouldn't doze off before the beverage service. I typically tried to stay away from too many carbs, but who can resist a cookie?

I was feeling rather nostalgic that day. There was something about the focus being back on me. By this time tomorrow I'd likely be having breakfast in the hotel lobby with my family and my sorors, laughing and reminiscing about old times and gearing up for my once-in-a-lifetime celebration.

We were very close and I loved them all, but a few years back you wouldn't know it. Some didn't understand my unconventional way of having a child. At the age of forty-seven, I became a MOBY, Mommy Older Baby Younger. I coined this phrase for women over the age of thirty-five who become first-time moms, or for those who may have older children but choose to start over.

The beauty of living your own life is that not everyone has to understand. No matter how many times you share your story with others, it is only you who lives it, breathes it, and feels it. So, at the end of the day, if the choice you make satisfies you and God, then you know you're on the right track.

The flight attendants were doing their demonstration, the one where nobody pays attention. I noticed a woman sitting across from us struggling with a fidgety baby. I smiled and gave her a wink.

"I know the feeling," I said. The woman politely smiled and gave a nod. A few years ago, this scenario would have devastated me. Even now, I will myself not to go down memory lane—thoughts of longing for something that you can't have.

"Please secure your mask before helping others," the flight attendant said. In other words, you can only help somebody else if you have yourself together. If only I had learned that sooner.

I felt myself drifting off, and I knew it was only a matter of time before I started watching my eyelids. The last sound I heard was the cry of a baby, and then the memories began to roll.

## CHAPTER 2

# LETTING GO

Scottsdale, Arizona, was beautiful. It's always nice when your company appreciates your hard work, especially when they send you and your sales team to a five-star resort. It wasn't Vegas, but I still say, "What happens in Scottsdale, stays in Scottsdale."

But even with all the amenities and creature comforts, my heart was heavy. I knew that trip would be the day I asked my vice president to make a personnel change, and that personnel change was me. At that time, I was married to Reggie, but he and I had finally realized that our marriage was in trouble, so I needed to convince her that I was the best person to fill the open sales position in Atlanta, Georgia. I was currently living in North Carolina. I had a stellar work ethic and made a good name for myself, but I knew that most times when a new job opens, there's already someone considered.

I'd rehearsed how I'd sell myself, my tenure at the company, my skill set, and proven track record. Surprisingly, the discussion was quick. She loved the idea, and thought I was ready to move on and move up. I did let the cat out of the bag about my legal separation, and that may have sealed the deal. After all, she'd previously gone through something similar.

So, after more prayers, counseling, and coming to terms with the fact that our marriage was irreparable, Reggie and I decided to take one of the most significant and painful steps of all—we decided to officially end our marriage.

The relocation package helped us sell the house. There was no settlement or alimony to consider since, unfortunately, after eleven years of marriage, we'd hardly accumulated anything to dispute, not even children. I was now on my way to Atlanta.

The emotional difficulty was the hardest part once I arrived in my new city. Divorce is like a death, and I'd died by a thousand slow cuts. Like any death, initially, you have the benefit of family and friends calling you, comforting you, and showering you with their presence. But after a while, it's understandable that those pillars of strength can only remain with you for an appointed time. After all, they have lives too.

Sure, I smiled on the outside, but that was after the antidepressant had kicked in. On the inside, I was a walking ball of pain, languishing in the misery of divorce. Every song, every TV show, and every movie would remind me of Reggie. I prayed every day for God to ease the pain. I found a church home, read books, recited scripture, read and reread uplifting cards from family and friends, and I even hung affirmations all around the house. I did anything to keep my pain at bay, but other sources added to that pain. One was my financial situation.

Reggie and I had been knee deep in debt—maxed-out credit cards, second mortgage, and believe it or not, payday loans. So even with the relocation package, I was barely getting by. We had robbed Peter, but still couldn't pay Paul, and I was dodging creditors and mortgage companies. My credit was so weak that, just to rent a townhome, I had to beg the couple to take a chance on me. Many people face financial hardships, but our challenges were not due to unemployment, nor were they due to overspending. I had worked every day, moving upward in my career and making money, but the power of addiction was stronger than both of us. Today, there seems to be more openness and resources that address this disease, but during our struggle, addiction was a dirty, nasty word, something that we chose to keep secret.

For eleven years, I hid Reggie's disease from friends and family, and shouldered it alone. We seemingly had the perfect marriage, but when I finally faced the facts, I realized that I was part of the problem. I was standing in the way of Reggie's deliverance. I was his crutch, and I was the textbook description of an enabler. I cleaned up all the messes, created and participated in all the lies, and I hid all the bodies. I was the Olivia Pope of our household, never allowing Reggie to hit bottom.

It was Reggie who ultimately made the decision that he needed time away from me. I'd even left the door open for him to join me in Atlanta, but we both knew that the abuse, both mentally and physically at times, was too much for either of us to continue our marriage.

## CHAPTER 3

# IT HAPPENED AGAIN

The other source of my pain was the burden of being barren. I was in my midthirties and single again. I had already accepted that with my track record, there was slim to no chance of me ever becoming someone's mom.

It had been four years since my most recent loss, but it seemed like only yesterday. I had gotten pregnant again. Reggie and I couldn't have been happier. We saw this as a sign things were finally turning around for us. Reggie's sobriety appeared to be holding fast. We'd prayed day and night that we wouldn't relive the torment of the previous pregnancy.

Prior to this last pregnancy, I was diagnosed as having an incompetent cervix. The protocol was that I'd have a cerclage at around twelve weeks. After some light spotting at only nine weeks, I immediately went to see Dr. Fallon.

"We'll need to move forward with the cerclage now, as there are already some changes in your cervix," she explained.

"Will I be able to carry this one to term?" I hesitantly asked.

"Well, changes in the cervix this early can be challenging, but I'll do all I can for a successful outcome." Dr. Fallon performed the procedure, and eight weeks later, things seemed to be going well. Each day my bundle remained inside of my body was a miracle. But, somehow, I knew that morning was different.

I awoke just before Reggie left for work. I'd felt the familiar twinges in my right side; fear and panic filled my mind. I slowly walked to the bathroom. Considering my track record for losses, checking the tissue always made me anxious. I wiped slowly. I paused before peering down, and as I looked, the sight of bright-red blood looking back at me almost stopped my heart.

After being admitted into the hospital, I was sure this was my last chance to become a mother. As much as I prayed to cradle a baby, my baby, in my arms, if things didn't work out this time, it wasn't meant to be.

I was just shy of my fifth month. I'd had the stitch this time, taken it easy, was on bedrest, and was seemingly doing everything right. This pregnancy had to come to fruition. I'd weathered the pain of multiple pregnancy losses and supported my husband through the challenges of addiction. I'd been a great aunt and godmother too. Wasn't it my turn? The answer was no—not this time.

As I lay there numb and completely in shock, Dr. Fallon walked into the room.

"Kimberly, we have to turn you in a Trendelenburg position, which is pretty much upside down. This position is our only chance of saving the pregnancy," she said as she tried to keep her cool. I just looked at her, tears in my eyes. I was frozen. Reggie sat in the only chair in the room. It was hard for us to look at each other. I felt he blamed me. Of all the women he could have married, he chose me, a woman who couldn't do what I thought real women were meant to do. That's not what he said, but that's how I felt.

Only one day had gone by since being admitted into the hospital. I started to get sick; the vomiting was uncontrollable. A young nurse named Salma attended to me. She would come into my room periodically to listen to the baby's heartbeat. This time, when she listened, I could hear a pinging sound, but this sound was not the same as what I'd previously heard with the doppler. The look on her face gave her away.

"Is everything okay?" I said, my voice trembling.

"I'm going to call the doctor," she said hurriedly. What seemed like hours was only minutes.

The doctor ordered an ultrasound. Once the machine was in my room, Dr. Fallon made her way to see me. The gel applied to my growing belly was usually extremely cold, but today I felt nothing. Dr. Fallon ran the paddle over my tummy, looking for movement. The technician who delivered the ultrasound machine and Salma stood by like nervous children. Reggie had left the hospital for work but was on alert should anything change. Dr. Fallon continued rolling about the paddle, shaking my tummy, and looking into the ultrasound machine.

Finally, she turned to me and said it. She said the words I'd heard during every pregnancy I'd attempted.

"I'm so sorry," she said.

I sat there, stone faced, eerily calm. No one would know the additional cracks that had just splintered my heart. I looked beyond Dr. Fallon. This time my heart had been guarded. This time I hadn't thought of names. I'd kept a piece of my heart to myself, not giving it all away. I already knew the drill. It was just the previous year that I'd experienced my longest pregnancy and my biggest loss with Elijah. I knew the worst part came next.

I'd soon have to deliver the baby.

It was time. Reggie watched intently. As I felt the baby leave my body, my eyes met Reggie's. He mouthed the words, "It's a boy." I didn't want to see him, not after what I'd gone through with Elijah a year before. I knew I had failed another child; I didn't feel like I deserved that moment. The pain was too much to bear.

Although Reggie had made it back for the delivery, he decided that he needed to go home for a change of clothes.

His parting words stung more than his absence. "Everybody has children. Why do we keep finding ourselves in the same place?" he cried.

As I lay there in pain, both physically and mentally, thoughts of my demise at my own hand played over and over in my head.

Through my tears, I questioned God, but I also blamed myself.

"I'm sorry, little one. If only you'd had a better vessel."

That night, my blood pressure began to drop fast, and the doctors weren't quite sure what was going on. Dr. Fallon had been checking in on me throughout the evening. She'd had some concerns about my blood pressure, but nothing that gave her alarm. Besides, she'd given me an epidural and other pain medications, so she attributed it to the medicine. Then, out of nowhere, the room filled with doctors. They drew blood from all over my body.

"Kimberly, we're checking you for sepsis!" one older, heavy-set nurse said in what seemed like a panic. Reggie hadn't returned yet, and I was just too out of it to make any real decisions. About an hour later, they wheeled me out into the hallway.

"We're taking you for emergency surgery," Dr. Fallon said in a hurried voice. As she spoke, a familiar face walked up. Joanne, a nurse who attended my church, had seen my name on the patient's list and immediately came to check on me.

"Her husband is not here," Dr. Fallon stated before she could utter a word. Joanne agreed to try to contact him and promised to make a call to our pastor.

Things ran a hundred miles an hour, but through the haze, I do remember blinking through the tears and asking Dr. Fallon, "Will I have to have a hysterectomy?"

She looked me in the eye. "If you wake up and you've had a hysterectomy, just please know we did all we could."

That was the last thing I remember before I woke up. Upon opening my eyes, the first person I saw was Dr. Fallon. She gave me the thumbs-up sign and whispered, "No hysterectomy."

Joanne quickly rushed in moments later. She hugged me and told me I'd given everyone a scare, but I instinctively looked around for Reggie.

"Where is my husband?" I asked.

"I haven't seen him," Joanne whispered. "I'm sure he'll be back soon." I knew he'd be back, but I also knew that he couldn't deal with this situation. I must have fallen asleep again because when I woke up, my pastor and his wife were sitting in chairs in front of me. The look on their faces spoke of love and sympathy. They'd been down this road with me before.

"Hi," was all I could muster. I had no energy. Pastor and Miss Linda both walked over to the bed.

"Hey Kimmy," Pastor said, calling me by the nickname he'd given me. He kissed me on the forehead, and Miss Linda bent down and hugged me with one of those hugs that wanted to take all the pain away.

"How are you feeling?" He knew the answer, but I could tell he was trying his best to console me. "We just spoke with Reggie. He's on his way," he said softly. Our eyes connected. We all knew that Reggie could not deal with this situation without a crutch. Situations like this catapulted him deeper into his addiction. As much as I wanted a child, needed a child, it was at times like this that I knew in my heart of hearts the relationship Reggie and I shared was no place for one. I'd always prayed that my child would have the benefits that I had growing up, particularly two loving parents who taught me to thrive. I knew Reggie had demons of his own to battle, so I felt like I couldn't expect him to battle mine too.

A nurse entered the room then. "Hello, Kimberly. I'm here to check your vitals, and I also need to check your bleeding." My pastor stepped out of the room, but I asked Miss Linda to stay.

Dr. Fallon walked into the room. "You gave us quite a scare," she said with a look of concern.

"So I heard," I responded. "Dr. Fallon, this is the first lady of my church, Miss Linda," I introduced.

"I just met your pastor in the hallway." She smiled.

"What happened? I know I lost the baby," I said as the tears began to flow, "but what caused the other concerns?"

"After the delivery, there was still a piece of the placenta attached to your uterus," she sighed. "You were bleeding out, so that's why I told you if you woke up, and you'd had a hysterectomy, please know that we did all we could."

"Well, thank you, Jesus!" shouted Miss Linda.

"Thank you, Jesus," I said in a low voice.

"We originally thought you had become septic," Dr. Fallon continued to explain, "but the test showed the infection was localized in the uterus. Once I did the ultrasound, I could see the spot where the placenta had not detached."

"Thank you," was all I could say. I was numb.

News of another loss traveled fast, and the phone calls started pouring in.

"Don't cry, Mom. It's okay," I told her as I held back my tears. I found myself having to reassure my family and friends over and over that I would be okay.

"Daddy, I'm fine. No, you don't need to fly down."

"Hey, sis, thank you so much. Just pray for me."

"Girl, I understand. It will be okay. I'm fine."

That's pretty much how every call went. I stayed in the hospital another night, and my close friends and colleagues, Tina and Xavier, stopped by along with some of the deacons from the church.

When asked, I told them Reggie was on his way, but they all knew the truth.

That night, the pain of the loss hit hard. Somewhere inside, my loins throbbed, the blood felt as if it were gushing, and the gas after the surgery caused my stomach to swell painfully. I lay there in bed, in the darkness, all alone. I spoke to the only person who could help me. I spoke to the Lord.

"Lord, this feels like the lowest moment in my life. I've lost another child, my husband is MIA, and my heart is heavy again from the pain of loss. Although the tears are streaming down my face, and as bad as I feel, I want you to know that I trust you and I love you. Nothing happens that you don't allow, and just like you got me through so many other devastating times in my life, I know you'll get me through this loss too."

This prayer will always be one of the highest points of my life. I praised God in the midst of my storm.

## CHAPTER 4

# WHAT'S UP, DOC?

It had been about six months since I'd separated with Reggie and moved to Atlanta, and things were starting to look up. I'd set myself up on a payment plan, and the salary from the new job allowed me to finally start putting a dent in my debt. My place was coming together nicely, and I was learning my way around the new city. One thing I left out was the hiccup that occurred after I initially relocated. Reggie went MIA before signing the divorce papers. I had to secure an attorney, take out an ad in his last known state, and request he contact me. After thirty days and no contact, my divorce was official. When I saw the actual divorce decree, it made me question my decision, but not for long. I knew it was for the best.

I had connected with Annette, my only family member I had in Georgia at the time, and my sorority sister, Vapes, who I'd known back in my hometown of Bloomfield, Connecticut. Between the two of them and my colleagues, I was starting to get out of the house. There was so much to do in Atlanta—museums, theaters, concerts, sports, nightlife, you name it. Atlanta, or the ATL for short, had it all.

I'd snagged some pretty good Chastain tickets on a few occasions through work. Earth, Wind & Fire and Al Jarreau come to mind at first, but the biggest pastime in the South is food.

In the South, they love to eat. Food, glorious food! I must have gone to every restaurant imaginable, and my waistline had started to show it. I couldn't work out fast enough or hard enough to keep my weight at bay. I started as a size six and moved into a size ten in what seemed like weeks.

Finally, all that Atlanta fun caught up to me. I felt completely run down, like something wasn't quite right. It was then I realized I needed to see a doctor, in-network of course. After all, my profession was Insurance Sales. I'd previously gone back to North Carolina to tie up some loose ends on the house and get a few more refills on my antidepressant, but this time I knew I needed to see someone local.

I went online to my employer portal and started looking for doctors in the Alpharetta area. To this day, I'm not sure how I decided. It may have been proximity, but more than likely, it was fate. For some reason, the name Dr. David Gowdy stood out, so I picked up the office phone and dialed. I remember a welcoming voice answering the phone.

I barely caught the name of the practice, but I responded once I heard the receptionist ask, "How may I help you?"

"Hello, this is Kimberly. With whom am I speaking?" I asked.

"My name is Roxanne," she politely replied.

"I'd like to make an appointment to see Dr. Gowdy," I said.

After gathering some personal information and checking several dates and times that worked for me, we finalized the appointment.

After giving her the last bit of information, she promised to email the paperwork over right away so I could complete it before my appointment.

"I look forward to seeing you," she said.

"Thank you," was all I could muster. I was feeling numb.

I decided to work from home on the day of the appointment. I knew I had a few proposals to get out that morning, but I wasn't feeling well. Everything seemed to move in slow motion. Fortunately for me, my doctor's appointment was that afternoon. I hadn't completed one page of the paperwork from Roxanne; I don't think anyone ever does.

On my way to their office, I got a call from my mom. She was notorious for phone calls. She had and still managed to call each of us almost daily. Right now, I was at the top of her list. Between my divorce, relocation, and debt crisis, she'd visited and phoned more often than usual.

"Hello Mom," I answered, trying to sound as upbeat as possible.

"Hey babe, how are you?"

"I'm doing well," I said as I suddenly coughed uncontrollably.

"Oh no, are you getting sick?" she asked in a tone that sounded like she was talking to a toddler.

"I'm on my way to the doctor's office now," I said. "It's probably a cold or maybe allergies. From what I hear, Georgia is famous for allergies."

"Well, call me as soon as you leave the office and tell me what they said," she demanded.

"Okay Mom, will do. I love you."

"I love you too, babe," she said in a concerned mother's voice. Hearing her voice always brought me comfort. Moms have a way of making things better.

I arrived at the doctor's office much faster than expected, but arriving earlier gave me some time to complete the paperwork. I pulled up to the quaint office complex and gave myself a quick face check in the mirror. I'd been coughing and blowing my nose so much that I had to make sure my face showed no visible evidence.

From the outside of the building, my first impression was that I'd made the right decision on a local doctor, but unfortunately, it's not what things look like on the outside that matter.

I entered a small medical office and immediately saw the reception area. Two women turned their heads in unison. I was sure one of them was Roxanne.

"Hello," greeted the younger woman. She looked to be in her late twenties or early thirties. She smiled as I approached the counter. Just then, the phone rang. "Just give me one second," she asked, the smile still projected on her face.

As I waited for her call to end, my peripherals caught sight of a gentleman sitting to my right. He wore a doctor's coat and appeared to be making notations.

"Sorry about that," the young receptionist finally said, drawing my attention back to her. "How may I help you?"

"I'm Kimberly Garrett. I have a two o'clock appointment to see Dr. Gowdy."

The gentleman turned around, and our eyes met. We exchanged pleasantries, I gently nodded my head, and he did the same. I wondered if he was Dr. Gowdy. The receptionist scrolled her perfectly manicured finger down the list of the day's patients.

"Yes, I see your name right here, Kimberly," she said.

"Are you Roxanne, by any chance?" I whispered.

"YES, I am!" she proudly shouted. She handed me a clipboard with what looked to be about ten pages of paperwork, then asked for my insurance card and ID. I gave my information to her and picked up the clipboard. Clearly, she knew I hadn't completed the paperwork beforehand.

As I made my way to my seat, a sinking feeling seeped into my belly. At this point, I'd seen the prominence of Atlanta, especially with African Americans. I'd closed business deals, and I'd entertained and socialized with some pretty heavy hitters in the ATL. Unfortunately, my self-esteem was still pretty low. I knew my past. I knew I was damaged. I had looked at this doctor and thought, *A person like him would never be interested in someone like me.* Unfortunately, this self-deprecating feeling lingered. But it wasn't about him specifically, but someone of his stature, someone who seemingly had it all together. He was, after all, a doctor.

As I started the paperwork, the doctor stood and started giving instructions to the receptionist who wasn't Roxanne. I noticed the gold band on his left hand, and all I could imagine was that his life was amazing—a beautiful wife and children without a care in the world.

I returned my attention to the paperwork. I was in pretty

good health overall and checked N/A for just about everything, but I dreaded the questions about surgeries. I'd had too many to count. I decided to leave that part blank. Today was a cold or allergies appointment, not an OB-GYN visit.

"Here you go." I handed the paperwork back to the receptionist.

"Thank you. The doctor will be with you shortly," she said with a smile.

After a brief wait, I was ushered back to see the doctor. Before we got to the room, the nurse stopped at the scale. If you think I dreaded the surgery questions, I loathed this part. After seeing my weight, I quickly made the nurse aware that the scale needed to be recalibrated. She laughed as we continued to the examination room.

"So, what is the reason for your visit?" she asked.

"I've been feeling run down, coughing, and sneezing," I replied. She took my vitals and told me the doctor would be with me shortly. I was doing my second stint of waiting, sitting on the exam table draped in that loud white crepe paper, waiting for the doctor to knock on the door. They always knock on the door first. What exactly do they think you could be doing in there? Even the OB-GYN knocks. Maybe they don't want to see you naked just before they make you spread-eagle and view everything from the rooter to the tooter.

Finally, I heard the knock as the door opened. The doctor with the beautiful gold wedding band was indeed Dr. Gowdy. He was a slim, bearded man with a thick mustache, a caramel complexion, and a bald head. He appeared to be in his early fifties and looked extremely serious, with glasses that sat low under his brown eyes.

"Hello, uh, Kimberly," he said as he quickly looked down to scan my chart. Not the warmest greeting. He got right to business. "So, I see you've had some respiratory problems," he said dryly. "How long has this been going on?"

"It's been a couple of weeks now," I said. "I just haven't been feeling myself. I've been feeling run down, and I've had a stuffy nose, headache, and constantly clearing my throat," I continued. The doctor made notes as I spoke.

After relinquishing the clipboard, he pulled a small flashlight out of his pocket and examined my eyes and throat. "Hmm," he said before pressing his stethoscope against my chest and back and asking me to breathe in and out slowly, and to breathe naturally.

"Based on your vitals and from what I can see, you appear to have an upper respiratory tract infection. I can have the nurse call in a prescription for an antibiotic. You should start to feel better in a couple of days, but make sure you finish all the medication," he instructed. "Also, your last doctor is listed in North Carolina."

"That's correct. I relocated from High Point," I explained.

"Do you plan on seeing someone locally?"

"Yes, that was my reason for coming to see you," I said sarcastically.

"Oh," he chuckled, then his disposition seemed to soften. "What brings you to Atlanta?"

"My job," I said with a smile.

"I assume you live in the area then. People either live or work wherever they see the doctor," he guessed.

"For me, it's both. I live and work in Alpharetta. The word on the street is that it's wise to live close to where you work, as the traffic can be relentless."

He vehemently nodded his head in agreement. "You'd better believe it. So, what do you do for a living?" he continued.

"I work in insurance sales." I beamed. I was so proud of my new position. Regardless of my failures everywhere else, my career had always been a bright spot.

"What's the reason for the antidepressant?" His question changed my countenance. I'd forgotten I'd listed it on my paperwork.

"Well, um, uh, I'd started taking it during my divorce," I nervously stated.

"And how long has that been?" he asked. His questions were back to their original direct and no-nonsense manner.

"About six months," I said. "I don't plan to refill it once I finish the last prescription," I said.

"That's not a good idea. You need to be weaned off of antidepressants, and it's best that you speak to someone who can guide you through the reason you needed them in the first place."

"It's a long story," I sighed, "but I think I'll be fine." He could see that I was uncomfortable with the direction the conversation had taken.

"I'll tell you what; there are some great doctors to help you with your situation. I refer patients all the time. I'll have DeNece give you the list." He was very matter of fact. I guess DeNece was the nurse who would also be responsible for having the scale recalibrated.

"Thank you so much. I'll be sure to call if needed," I sighed.

"There's nothing wrong with seeking mental health advice," he said. "That's a common misconception, especially with African Americans." He gave his commentary as he picked up the clipboard, jotted down some additional notes, and walked out of the room. As I made my way to the front desk, I could hear Dr. Gowdy directing DeNece to make sure I had a follow-up appointment for one week.

My next appointment arrived quickly. I assumed it would be easy breezy. I was feeling much better; the antibiotic had done its job. Once I arrived, I went through the same motions, except this time, there was no paperwork. The scale was still flawed, but other than that, I expected it to be a great visit. I heard the knock on the door as Dr. Gowdy walked in.

"So, how are you feeling?" he asked.

"Great," I exhaled. He went through the motions of my previous visit, using his flashlight and stethoscope to examine me and asking me to breathe in and out.

"Sounds great." He beamed. I had a very different appointment compared to the last.

"Did you call any of the doctors from the list?" he asked.

"No, I just haven't had the time, but I still plan to call," I lied.

"What about family? Do you have relatives here?" he asked.

"I have a cousin here and a good friend, but my family is in Connecticut."

His ears seemed to perk up at this news. "So, you're a Northerner?"

"Yes." I beamed with pride.

"I'm from New Jersey myself." He smiled.

"My best friend lives in Trenton," I said excitedly.

As we conversed, I learned of his Jamaican heritage. He had a wife, two daughters, and he loved to salsa dance. His life was exactly as I expected. I'm sure his impression of me was just as stellar. I was divorced, childless, and in need of a shrink.

In all, I thought I'd made a great choice with Dr. Gowdy. He seemed to know his stuff. I now officially had a primary care physician.

## CHAPTER 5

# WELCOME TO ATLANTA

The move to Atlanta proved to be just what the doctor ordered. The depression was slowly dissipating and I was starting to feel like my old self.

Every Monday, a group of us would talk in the break room about our weekend, children, dating, etc. But I never had much to contribute. Sure, I was ready to explore more than museums and theaters, but I never seemed to meet anyone that captured my attention. One night, Vapes called. Her go-to spot was the Snoots in Buckhead on a Friday night, and she wanted me to join her. The Snoots, a high-end hotel with a restaurant and lounge, was where she and the who's who of the ATL would congregate. I'd tagged along a couple of times, but everyone seemed so stuffy at this hot spot.

At the time, I drove a modest sedan, was digging myself out of debt, and had put on twenty extra pounds. I was hardly a who's who, but I was happier than I'd been in years.

"So, what time are we talking?" I asked.

"Let's get there about 8:30," she replied. "That way, we can get a table before the crowd comes." She sounded so sure of herself.

"Okay, I'll be ready."

As I got dressed, I stopped and stood in front of the mirror. I was happy with the woman staring back at me. Sure, I'd gained some weight, but, in my mind, I'd lost the weight of the world, and it felt good.

That summer, I'd had so many visitors. Family members made their way down to the ATL. Sometimes there were so many that we called it a family reunion. I'd even spoken with Reggie a few times. He was on the right track now, and boy was I glad to know that.

I heard the doorbell. Unfortunately, I wasn't quite ready. I hoped that I'd dressed okay as I rushed down the stairs. After giving myself a once-over, I opened the door. Vapes looked as stunning as ever. She wore a black, off-the-shoulder dress and gold, strappy sandals with a black purse clutched under her arm. Suddenly, I felt underdressed.

"Hey girl, how you doin'?" she playfully asked.

"I'm good, and I'm almost ready. I just need to decide on shoes and jewelry." Now that I'd seen her attire, I knew I needed to step it up. It was too late to change the brown fitted dress, but the extra jewelry and higher heels would do the trick.

Ten minutes later, we headed out the door. As we made our way down my walkway, I could see her shiny white luxury sedan parked directly in front of my townhome. Whenever we hit the town, she always chose to drive, so I took it that my car didn't fit the occasion.

Vapes whipped down Georgia 400 at record speed. Her car drove so much smoother than mine. I noticed the speedometer read eighty. At eighty mph, my eleven-year-old sedan would have been shaking.

"I need to stop at an ATM," Vapes said. We were getting off the Lenox exit.

"Do you need change for the valet?" I asked. "If so, I have cash."

"That's exactly why I needed to stop," she replied.

"Have you heard of this place called Shakers?" I asked.

"Yes, it's right across the street from the Snoots. Do you want to go there instead?"

"Well, maybe just for a minute so I can say I've been to another spot in the ATL." The truth was that I'd heard that Shakers was more laid-back and much less stuffy than the Snoots.

We approached Phipps Plaza, an upscale shopping mall in Buckhead. Parking was a nightmare. We watched a couple exiting one of the establishments, and hoped they remembered where they parked. I hate following someone who then suddenly realizes they're two aisles over.

We were in luck. We saw the light flash on the car just ahead and took the spot as they left. Once we made our way into Shakers, the atmosphere was just as I'd hoped. The room was dim and plastered with big-screen televisions and high-top tables. The diverse crowd created just the right atmosphere for me, with people sitting in clusters laughing and talking over a glass of their favorite adult beverage.

"Hey, let's grab those two seats over there." Vapes had spotted two seats at the bar. I felt more at home in this environment. Don't get me wrong, I loved the maturity of the Snoots, but like Sammy Davis Jr. says, "I gotta be me."

The Snoots was right across the street, so I knew it wouldn't be long before Vapes tired of Shakers. Still, for the moment, I was enjoying the atmosphere as I people-watched and had a light conversation with a guy named Kiwan, who just happened to be sitting next to me.

At this point, I was a year out from my divorce, and I was open to possibilities.

"Are you from Atlanta?" Kiwan asked.

"No, Connecticut," I answered. "How about you?"

I seemed hard-pressed to meet anyone who was from Atlanta. We all seemed to be transplants. The conversation continued, but nothing about this person interested me. There was so much pretense in Atlanta. Every person in Atlanta was a millionaire or friends with millionaires or knew somebody who knew somebody who was a millionaire.

I loved the atmosphere at Shakers, but I couldn't get away from Kiwan fast enough, plus the look on Vapes' face told me she was ready to pack it up.

Against my better judgment, I'd let her talk me into trying an apple martini. I'm a red-wine-only girl, so needless to say, when I stood up I was feeling a little off-kilter, and the night was still young.

Unlike Shakers, finding a parking spot at the Snoots was the least of our worries; it was valet only. The atmosphere was diverse, same as Shakers, but slightly older and a lot more upscale.

We casually strolled through the lobby and made our way over to the streaming jazz music. The songstress had that Anita Baker meets Diane Krall type voice; it was serious. Our stop at Shakers had jeopardized any hopes of getting a table up close, so we decided to stand off in a corner—Vapes with her signature martini and me with red wine.

After a while, an older gentleman approached me. He looked to be in his midfifties with salt-and-pepper hair and a deep brown complexion. He invited us to join him and the rest of his friends. I was a little nervous, but considering I had only worn these strappy sandals once, my feet were crying out for relief.

"I'm Morris," he introduced.

"Kimberly," I nervously replied. Vapes was the social butterfly. She conversed with the entire group, but I found myself only talking to Morris.

What started as a casual meeting at the Snoots quickly turned into a budding relationship. Morris introduced me to the finer things—five-star restaurants, the arts, an entire echelon of people I would otherwise have no interest in meeting, etc. I enjoyed this world much more than I expected. I made changes to my appearance, highlighted my hair, upped my wardrobe, and shed about twenty pounds. I fit right into this new world of 7-series luxury cars, courtside Falcon tickets, and lavish trips, and I enjoyed every moment.

Still, I'd hoped to remarry someday. I just wasn't the perpetual dating type. I knew I wanted more. The way I saw it, once you've reached a certain age, it really shouldn't take long to know if you want to spend the rest of your life with someone.

So, six months into the relationship, I started throwing hints. "So, can you see us together years from now?" I hinted.

"Who knows where we might be years from now," he always deflected. "Let's just enjoy the now." But I continued to throw those subtle hints until I grew tired of the game. There were other hints and one situation not so subtle that led me to conclude that Morris may not be the one for me.

The not-so-subtle hint came when I saw him at a concert at Chastain with the woman he'd previously told me was an old friend. We'd bumped into her a few times during the relationship, and each time I saw her, things just seemed off.

I was about to approach them when I noticed she was actually feeding him. I had male friends myself, but I didn't feel comfortable feeding any of them unless they were in a hospital bed, and even then, I might call a nurse. I watched them the entire time, and I couldn't help but follow behind her after I saw her and a friend make their way toward the ladies room. I listened intently.

"Morris and I are in a good place," she said.

"I see," her friend commented.

"We have our friends, but we always come back to each other," she said. I thought I'd be devastated, but I didn't care as much as I should have.

When I made my way back to my seat, I made sure Morris saw me. The look on his face was priceless. I quickly realized that I enjoyed my time with him, but seemingly that time was over. I don't think I was ever in love with him, but I certainly enjoyed the excitement he brought to my life. At least that's what I told myself.

## CHAPTER 6

# HOME SWEET HOME

I had all but paid off most of my debt. I loved renting my townhome, but I was considering buying a home of my own. I knew my landlord was interested in selling his townhome to me, but I needed something new. I'd come to Atlanta as a caterpillar, I had shed my cocoon in this home, and I wanted to leave it there.

The housing market was red hot. New subdivisions were going up everywhere. I knew the short sale from my previous life was still showing on my credit report, but with my substantial income I hadn't missed a payment in over a year. I could at least start looking. I assumed I had more time to look for a new home, but shortly after I expressed disinterest in buying my current townhome, I found out the owner had decided to sell it. They declined my offer to rent month to month and gave me two months to vacate. This news lit a fire under me.

Vapes offered her home as a backup, as there was no way I could find a place, close on it, and move in, all in two months' time. Knowing I had a place to fall back on was a blessing.

With so much uncertainty about my living arrangement, I figured purchasing a P.O. box was the best thing to do for starters. As soon as I walked into the post office, I spotted a familiar face.

"Hey, Dr. Gowdy, how are you?" I greeted him in an exaggerated voice.

He looked up from his mail. "Hey there," he said, seeming a little confused.

"It's me, Kimberly Garrett, your patient." He finally recognized me.

"Oh, how have you been?" he asked.

"I've been fine," I answered. "I just made an appointment to see you for my physical." I felt proud that I was taking my health seriously.

"Good to hear," was his response. "You work in insurance, right?" he asked.

"Yes, how did you remember?" I was surprised.

"I always remember crooks," was his unexpected comeback.

"Are you kidding me? Doctors are the biggest crooks imaginable," I shot back. Our dialogue went back and forth for about ten minutes, and some of the patrons started to listen.

One lady, who reminded me of Sophia Petrillo from *The Golden Girls*, chimed into our conversation. "You tell her, Doctor. It's the insurance companies that are the greedy ones." I knew I'd lost this argument.

I completed my business, said my goodbyes, and kindly walked out of the post office, holding on to the last shred of dignity I had left.

The day of my physical came before I knew it, and I made sure it was first thing in the morning. The nurse said no eating after twelve the night before, and I try to eat most of my calories in the morning, so I wanted to get this over as soon as possible. I arrived at the office fifteen minutes early. Once DeNece called me back and directed me to the scale, I stepped up with confidence. I'd lost twenty-two pounds, and it felt good.

I sat in the exam room, waiting for Dr. Gowdy. I was going to bring up his manufactured argument in the post office. A knock sounded at the door, and Dr. Gowdy entered. When we made eye contact, we both burst into laughter.

"I'd better check you for bruising after that beatdown you endured the other day," he laughed.

"You started it," I joked.

"It was all in fun," he continued to laugh.

After my physical, he told me they'd be taking blood work. He wanted to make sure my A1C and vitamin D were okay. Diabetes had affected several of my family members, so I tried to stay on top of that.

"So, how are things going for you so far? Are you adjusting well to Atlanta?" he asked.

"Yes, the move here has been pretty good. I'm looking around for a new house because the owner is selling the rental property where I reside." I put on the woe-is-me look.

"There's a new garden home development going up off of Highway 9," he said. "They're beautiful. I just bought one."

"Well, Dr. Gowdy, anywhere you can afford to buy, I likely cannot afford," I said very matter-of-factly.

"I bought two, one to live in and one to rent," he said. I just assumed his family had decided to move, but then he blurted, "I'm divorced."

"Oh no, I'm so sorry to hear that," I said. I knew how painful things had been for me in the beginning. He was quick to change the subject.

"So, we'll be in touch with your results," he stated. "Assuming everything is okay, we'll see you back next year." He got up and left.

After I left the exam room, I stopped by the front desk to pay my copay, and Dr. Gowdy stood there making notes.

He looked up. "Here you go." He handed me a card with a name and an address. "Don't forget to take a look at the subdivision. I'm sure you'll like it," he repeated. I agreed, but I knew there was no way I could afford it.

I was doing well, but not doctor well.

I left the doctor's office and headed to the coffee shop for a venti white mocha. I deserved it; I was starving. I had already decided I wasn't going into the office, so since I was out, I decided to take a look at the subdivision, the one that had turned Dr. Gowdy into a walking advertisement. I didn't have anything to lose. I took out the card he'd given me and put the location in my GPS. Unfortunately, the address didn't come up. I dialed the number on the paper.

"Hello, Home Sales," a woman with a polite voice announced. I verified the subdivision address, but considering it was so new, it didn't register on my GPS. She was eager to get my contact information, then directed me to the area and told me she'd be in the office until five.

"I'm on my way," I said. Most of the homes in the quaint little subdivision had already gone up, but there was still one street left with a few aqua-blue poles sticking out of the ground. After driving around, I decided to park in front of the sales office.

As I walked toward the office, a tall, dark-haired woman exited the door. "Kimberly?" she asked.

"Yes, you must be Tatiana." I was sure of it.

The first model was nice, but not quite what I wanted. The second model blew me away! It had everything I wanted and more. I could envision all of my furniture in this place. The high ceilings, the oversized patio, and the loft were everything. It was perfect for entertaining. All I could hear as I walked from room to room were the voices of my parents. They'd be bursting with pride at how far I'd come if I secured this home. This home was mine. I had already claimed it.

As Tatiana and I walked back to the office, I did everything I could to show a lack of excitement, but she knew I liked what I saw. Fortunately for me, they only had five homes available since they were closing out the subdivision, and I received some free upgrades. Building the home would take four months. I knew I had to take Vapes up on her offer. I happily completed all the paperwork, and the final question on the page stood out like a neon sign.

"How did you hear about us?" I gladly wrote *Dr. David Gowdy* on the line. Little did I know that info would change my life.

## CHAPTER 7

# I DO

I'd gotten approved. Buying a home can be so stressful, especially a brand-new one. I had to pick out everything from the knobs to the flooring. When I initially heard "design center," I was excited, but in hindsight, it was overwhelming. Once I made the final decision, I was glad it was over. Now all I had to do was store my things and room with Vapes for the next three and a half months.

Time flew by, and before I knew it, I was sitting at my closing, signing my life away. Vapes joined me. Things between Morris and I had cooled off quite a bit, especially after what happened at Chastain. Since then, I'd only seen him a few times while I was living with Vapes. He'd arranged to have my things delivered to my new home. I appreciated it, but it seemed more of a friendly gesture than a committed relationship.

I'd been living in my new digs for about a month when my cell rang. I didn't recognize the number.

"Hello?" I answered.

"Hello, Kimberly?"

"Yes, may I ask who's calling?" I didn't recognize the voice.

"It's David."

"Who?"

"I'm sorry, Dr. Gowdy."

"Oh! Hi Dr. Gowdy, did I miss an appointment?" I asked.

"No, nothing like that. I'm calling to say thank you!"

"For what?" I was puzzled.

"Didn't you purchase a home in my subdivision?"

"Yes, how did you know?"

"Well, I just received a $500 check from the builder!"

"Really?" I asked, shocked.

"Yes, you listed me as a referral, and they sent me a referral fee," he laughed. "Who knew?"

"Well, don't thank me. That was the least I could do. I love my new place."

"Maybe I can take you to dinner?" He suggested.

"Well considering they did send you $500, that's the least that you can do," I joked. We both laughed.

I arrived at the restaurant shortly after 7:00 p.m. Dr. Gowdy sat casually in the waiting area. He wore a blue-and-white button-down shirt, khakis, and loafers. He looked up and gave me the warmest smile.

"I wasn't sure if you'd had second thoughts," was his response. He looked pleased to see me, and I must admit, I enjoyed this new scenery.

We walked to the reception area, and he alerted them that his party had arrived. They immediately escorted us to a large U-shaped booth. I sat close to the middle, and Dr. Gowdy sat close to me.

"So, how are things?" I asked.

"Things are good." He nodded. "Very busy, but I can't complain. How are things in the world of insurance?"

"Same ole, same ole," I replied. "I would say more, but I don't want to get into another debate with you." I had to say it. We both laughed. Things were going well. He ordered a bottle of red wine, we enjoyed appetizers, tasted each other's entrees, and laughed. Dinner was great. I hadn't had that much fun since the first week with Morris. It felt good to connect with someone.

About two weeks prior, I'd passed by Dr. Gowdy's home on my way to the store, and I saw him getting into a car with a woman. At the time I had thought about stopping to say hello, but I didn't want to look like a stalker, so I kept going. I figured this was his new love interest. It was none of my business, but since things seemed to be going so well this evening, I was looking for a subtle way to add it into our conversation.

"So, have you started dating at all since your divorce?" I finally blurted it out.

"I've been seeing someone, but it's not serious," he responded. "What about you?"

"I was dating someone and thought it was going somewhere, but things seem to be fizzling out,"

"Is it the guy with the black sedan?" he said coyly.

"Wait. What?" I couldn't believe it.

"A couple of times when I drove into the neighborhood, I passed by your home and saw it parked in your driveway," he said. At least I wasn't the only stalker.

Just then, his phone rang. He looked down, and his expression changed.

"I need to take this call," he said. "Dr. Gowdy," he announced, listening intently. I sensed something was wrong.

He disconnected the call. "I'm so sorry, but I'm going to have to cut this short. It's my mother."

"Oh no, is she okay?" I asked, genuinely concerned.

"I don't know. That was my mom's caregiver. She was rushed to the hospital." He motioned for the server to bring us the check. I suddenly felt sorry for him. "Yeah, I better get going," he said hastily.

"Do you want me to ride with you to the hospital?" I blurted.

"No, I couldn't ask you to do that."

"Really, it's okay."

"No, I'm fine." He quickly retrieved his credit card. Five minutes later, we were each getting back into our cars. I felt terrible for him. I sat in the car and said a prayer for his mom. I was hoping that she was okay.

No sooner than I pulled out of the parking lot, my phone rang.

"Hello?" I answered.

"Hey there, it's David. On second thought, I would like you to come to the hospital with me." David made his way back to the parking lot, scooped me up, and we headed to the hospital.

David and I walked into the emergency entrance of the hospital. He was familiar with most of the staff.

"Hi, Dr. Gowdy," a young woman sitting at the nurse's station said. He leaned in to speak to her, and then we walked over to a white curtain that doubled as a makeshift private room.

David slid the curtain back to find his mother, a petite, fair-skinned woman with soft brown eyes and a kind smile. Her face was riddled with pain.

"Hi Mom," he greeted. Before she could even return pleasantries with her son, her eyes made contact with mine.

"Who's she?" Her eyes stayed focused on me.

"This is Kimberly. Kimberly, this is my mother, Dorothy." I was intimidated, but I managed to keep my cool.

"Hello, Dorothy. Nice to meet you," I responded.

"She's pretty," was all she said. I knew they needed their privacy, so I opened the curtain and stepped out. I tried not to listen to the conversation, but I couldn't help myself.

"Where is Sharon?" she asked. "Are you still seeing her?"

"Mom, let's focus on getting you better," he said.

"I like her. She has kind eyes," his mom uttered.

By then, the doctor had come into the room, and they discussed his mom's condition. David requested that I come back into the room, and as I entered, he and the doctor left for further discussion.

As I stood in the room, I could feel Miss Dorothy's eyes on me.

"You're very pretty," she said. "I told David I like you." I walked closer to her bed just as the nurse entered the room. "My legs are in pain!" she yelled to the young heavy-set nurse.

"I'll let the doctor know," the nurse said as she exited the room. His mom winced in pain, so I slowly walked over to her and gently rubbed her hair.

"It's okay," I said. Our eyes met, and I smiled. "God will take care of you," I whispered. She shook her head in agreement.

"My legs," she whimpered. I made my way to the end of the bed, lifted the blanket, and began to massage her legs. She seemed to take comfort in my work, and I took comfort in knowing that I had clothed myself in humility.

"Thank you," she breathed. Once Dr. Gowdy returned to the room, there was a warmth that filled the air. We exchanged glances. I think we both knew that this was the start of something more.

The friendship between Dr. Gowdy and I grew. There wasn't a day that went by that we didn't converse. Living in the same subdivision made it easy for us to connect. After work, he'd either stop by to see me, or I'd make a beeline through my backyard to see him. We did this all under the guise of friendship. I knew Sharon was still part of his life and he knew that Morris was still present in mine, but the more time I spent with him, the more I realized I was falling for him.

Ultimately, my change became evident to Morris and we officially called it quits, but when I shared my news with Dr. Gowdy, he remained close-lipped about Sharon.

Time went on, and what started as a beautiful Sunday afternoon suddenly turned sad. I received a call from Dr. Gowdy.

"Hey you," I said. I always welcomed his calls.

"My mother died," he exhaled.

"I am so sorry to hear about your mom." I did my best to console him, and over the next several days, I was a friend, offering to be of service in any way possible.

At the repast, I got a chance to meet David's family—his two daughters, Angela and Gabrielle, and his ex-wife, Diana. Even divorced, he and Diana appeared to be close. I also had a chance to meet Sharon.

Dr. Gowdy had made his way over to my table, and a short, slender woman with a dark mocha complexion accompanied him. I stood and gave him a warm, gentle hug of support, and I made eye contact with the woman.

"Sharon, this is Kimberly. Kimberly, this is Sharon." David made introductions, and we exchanged pleasantries.

After the repast, I distanced myself. I knew that Dr. Gowdy and I were no more than friends, and I was fine with that. For the next several weeks, he and I had minimal conversation; I figured the pain of losing his mom had a lot to do with that.

One evening out of the blue, my doorbell rang. I peered out and saw Dr. Gowdy. I opened the door.

"Dr. Gowdy, what are you doing here?"

"I can't seem to get you on the phone," he uttered.

"I just figured you needed space," I said softly.

"I know what I need," he said. His comment threw me for a loop.

"How's Sharon?" I asked.

"I don't know. I'm not seeing her anymore," he said. Then, without warning, Dr. Gowdy leaned in and kissed me. After that first kiss, we were inseparable. We had become two people in love in just a short time.

We'd even started looking for rings, but that still didn't prepare me for the day David asked the one question that would alter the course of our lives forever.

One particular evening, out of nowhere, about five months into our relationship, I was standing in the loft of his home paying no mind to my surroundings when I heard rustling behind me. I turned around and David was on one knee.

"Oh no! Are you okay?" I blurted, genuinely concerned. There was a significant age difference between us, so I jokingly asked if one of his legs had given out. Then I noticed the box in his hand.

He opened the box without taking his eyes off me. "Will you be my wife?" he asked in the sweetest voice. With tears streaming down my face, I answered the only way I could.

"Of course."

He slid the ring on my finger, and I helped him up off the floor.

"I just have one request," he said.

"What's that?"

"Can you please stop calling me Dr. Gowdy?" We erupted with laughter.

We were married twice after that. Seven months later in our pastor's office, witnessed by Vapes and our two favorite church ladies, Ruby and Blanche, and then two months after that in Montego Bay, Jamaica, with family and friends.

David was the man that I'd prayed for, for what seemed like an eternity. He was everything I knew I wanted in a husband: God-fearing, successful, protective, and loving.

## CHAPTER 8

# ELIJAH

One morning, David and I decided to take a walk on the Alpharetta Greenway. All the walkers, joggers, and bike riders were out. As we walked, an adorable Asian family caught our eyes. They strolled just ahead of us. The dad pulled the two munchkins in a wagon, and the mom was walking by his side. We both smiled at the sight.

As we continued our walk, Dave casually turned to me and said, "That might be us one day."

"Might be us in what way?" I was baffled. "Are we going to become an Asian couple?" I joked.

"Might be us with children." He was serious. I had just assumed that the last thing David wanted was to start all over. He was more than ten years older than me, and he already had two grown children. It never even occurred to me that we'd be having this conversation. I guess that's what happens in whirlwind relationships; you forget to talk about the important things.

I always wanted children, and Lord knows I tried. But after six miscarriages and two late-term pregnancies, I believed that children weren't in God's plan for me.

After my pregnancy with Elijah, I had discovered I had an incompetent cervix. The sad thing about this condition is that you don't know you have it until you've lost or almost lost the baby. There are no warning signs. Your cervix simply succumbs to the weight of the baby.

When I was younger, I'd had an abortion. I know I'm not the only one who'd ever gone down this road, but after I'd encountered so much loss in this area of my life, there were times when I blamed myself for that decision. Maybe it was God's way of punishing me. It's not often that I feel this way, but when I do, the feelings rush in like a flood.

With my last pregnancy, I'd guarded my heart. I was prepared, stayed even-keeled, and didn't get too happy. I stayed just middle of the road. But Elijah had caught me off guard. I was hopeful. I laid it all out there for family and friends to experience my happiness, but my joy was short-lived. I had made it past the infamous twelve-week mark, and then the five-month mark, so I thought I was home free.

However, one night as I lay in bed, thinking about my baby, no doubt, a surge of warmth wrapped the lower part of my body.

*Did I just pee?* I thought to myself. I rose slowly, and once I stood, I could feel warm liquid trickling down my leg.

"Reggie! Reggie! I think something's wrong!" I panicked. I was out of my mind; I didn't know what to do. All my thoughts were running together. I didn't want to move too quickly for fear of hurting the baby, but I knew I needed to get to the hospital immediately.

Reggie and I made our way down Wendover Avenue. We were living in Greensboro, North Carolina, at the time. As we entered the emergency room, tears falling from my eyes, I screamed for someone to see me. Thank God it was a slow night, so they were able to take me back immediately.

I was rushed back to an exam room.

"So, tell me what's going on," the ER nurse asked.

"I woke up, and I thought I'd peed, but I knew I hadn't. I just need someone to help." I was rambling.

"Okay, how far along are you?" she asked as calmly as she could.

"I'm twenty-three weeks."

"Okay, lie back for me, and let's take a listen," she instructed. I lay back on the bed with Reggie at my side. After she squirted the gel onto my belly, she slowly moved the doppler over my belly to take a listen.

"Heartbeat sounds good," she said. That was hurdle number one. "I'll contact your doctor, but in the meantime, we're going to do a fern test and an ultrasound. This test will tell us if any amniotic fluid is leaking," she said. I was so paranoid that I was beside myself.

After what felt like days, the nurse knocked on the door and walked in.

"Good news, there's no sign of amniotic fluid loss. I ordered the ultrasound, but I spoke with the doctor, and since the heartbeat sounds good and there's no sign of amniotic fluid, we don't think there's any need for an ultrasound." I was ecstatic, thrilled. But that was all about to change.

Two days later, I woke up with the worst back pain imaginable. I stood under a hot shower, praying for relief. I called the doctor's office, and they told me someone from their practice would be waiting for me. I called Reggie and asked if he could come immediately. I was prepared to call an ambulance. Reggie arrived in record time.

Reggie and I pulled right up to the double doors of the emergency room. After finding me a seat, he ran over to the front desk.

"My wife is pregnant. Her doctor is Dr. Fallon. They said somebody would meet us here!" he blurted.

"Okay, sir, Dr. Ramsey is the doctor on call with that practice. I'll let them know you're here." A short, heavy-set nurse came out with a wheelchair. I was practically on the floor and sweating profusely. Reggie was asked to move his car, and he made it back just in time to go back with us.

Sitting on the table, waiting for the doctor to come in, I begged God to let everything be okay. The doctor, a petite African American woman, walked into the room along with the nurse who'd taken my vitals.

"Hello, Kimberly. I'm Dr. Ramsey," she greeted. "I'm going to do an exam and take a listen to the baby, okay?" Her voice was soothing. I was still in pain, sweating profusely, and had started to shake uncontrollably. The gel was applied, and it was now time to listen. We heard the heartbeat, but it was extremely slow. I knew this wasn't normal.

She finally had me put my feet in the stirrups to begin the examination.

After the exam, she stood up. "You can sit up now, sweetheart," she said and walked out of the room. I was confused. Reggie and I both looked at the nurse, but she looked just as confused as we were.

The doctor finally returned. "I'm sorry, but I'm afraid your membranes have ruptured," she announced. I must have looked confused.

She let out a breath, and her next words were measured and solemn. "Your water broke, Kimberly," she explained. "At only twenty-three weeks, there's little to no chance that the baby will survive."

"There is a chance!" I cried.

"When I examined you, Kimberly, I could already see the baby's footling," she explained further. "And judging from the heart rate, it's just a matter of time. Your temperature is a hundred degrees, and you're likely fighting an infection, which is why you're sweating."

I thought that hearing this news would send me off the deep end, but I gritted my teeth and continued rocking back and forth from the pain, with tears free-falling from my eyes.

"So, what now?" I cried.

"Again, I'm sorry," Dr. Ramsey said. "I'll have the nurse take you to a birthing room. We'll give you something for the pain." I could sense that her heart hurt for me.

As they wheeled me upstairs, I finally made eye contact with Reggie. His eyes were red and filled with tears. I imagined he hated me at this point. Once Reggie and the nurse helped me to bed, another nurse walked into the room.

"Hi, I'm Barbie. I'm here to set up your morphine drip. It will help with your pain." As she inserted the large needle into my hand, the doppler was used to take another listen. There was barely any sound at all. I began to cry uncontrollably.

The morphine must have put me to sleep. When I awoke, it was morning. Dr. Ramsey walked into the room.

"How are you feeling?" she asked. "It's time to get this show on the road." Her demeanor had taken on such a different tone. Nurse Barbie came back into the room.

"Hello, Kimberly. Are you ready to push?" she asked.

"Yes, I'm ready." Reggie quickly jumped off the cot.

"I'll drape a sheet over your legs if you don't want to see anything," Barbie offered. I nodded. After draping the sheet, she said, "You can start pushing as soon as you're ready."

I was nervous. My heart was racing. Nurse Barbie stood to my left, and Reggie stood to my right. It was time.

After about three pushes, I said, "I think he's out." Nurse Barbie lifted the sheet slightly.

"Oh my God," Reggie cried out. The nurse wrapped the baby in the sheet and handed him to Reggie. I initially thought seeing the baby would be too much to handle, but as I saw Reggie holding him gently in his arms, I reached for my baby. I placed him close to my bosom.

"My sweet Elijah," I cried, and my tears fell atop his tiny head. I unwrapped the sheet; I wanted to take in his tiny body. I kissed his fingers and counted his toes. I knew there would be no fanfare. No one would tell me how great I did. No cigars would be handed out. But none of that mattered. Nothing would change the fact that I was a mother. The pain, the grief, and the love that I felt at that very moment could only be a mother's love.

Unfortunately, after I gave birth, I had to have another dilation and curettage (D&C), which is the technical term for scraping the uterus. The doctor wanted to make sure all the placentae had detached. After I woke up from the surgery, I noticed that I was in another room. Reggie was watching television. The attending nurse came in to check on me.

"I think it would be a good idea to take a walk for circulation," the nurse suggested. She helped me out of bed, and upon opening the door, I noticed a white flower.

"Why the flower?" I asked. Her eyes looked away. "It's to alert any of the staff coming to your room that you've had a loss." Just then, an older couple who looked to be in their seventies stepped into the hall holding balloons and a teddy bear. They entered the room next to mine.

"There she is," I overheard them say. As I started my walk, I could hear laughter and loud talking, and see family members piled into rooms, smiling and hugging. I could hear the sound of a crying baby up ahead. I couldn't control my tears.

For the life of me, I couldn't understand why they had placed me on the maternity floor. It was like a bad movie. I stopped at the nurse's station. I know I must have looked like a mad woman.

"I just lost my baby, and this is the floor I get assigned?" I said, tight-lipped.

"Oh no, I'm sorry," the nurse behind the desk said. "Please tell me your room number."

"It's the room with the white flower."

Shortly after that, the head nurse came to see me.

"I am sorry for our insensitivity to your loss," she said.

I said nothing. I just lay in my bed with my back to her. I'd already told Reggie what had happened.

"I think you should leave," Reggie uttered.

The nurse again expressed her apologies. "Can I get you anything?" she asked. "Would you like something to drink?"

"Ma'am, would you like something to drink?" I heard a woman say as I stirred from my sleep. I looked up and saw a tall, slender flight attendant staring down at me.

"What?" I was confused.

"Would you like something to drink?" she repeated.

"Coffee," I replied.

I had drifted into my own world.

"Cream and sugar?" she asked.

"Just cream, and don't forget the cookies," I smiled. She passed two packs of cookies to me. David passed me the coffee. "Thank you." I nodded.

I looked at David. He was wearing his headset and playing sudoku in the back of the Sky Magazine. I pointed to my watch and mouthed, "How much longer?"

He lifted the headset off one ear and said, "Not sure. Maybe halfway. We sat on the runway forever." He went back to listening to smooth jazz, no doubt, and I enjoyed my refreshments.

"Mmmm, these cookies always do the trick."

Despite the coffee and cookies, sleep eventually overcame me again, and I found myself back on memory lane walking side by side with David just before we embarked on the hardest journey of our lives.

"So, do you think that might be us one day?" he asked.

"I think we need to talk," I mumbled. "I've always wanted children. I can't even express how much. But I've been down this road too many times, and each time ended in loss."

My eyes filled with tears. David could see that he'd hit a nerve. He stopped walking, grabbed my arm, and held me close.

"I'm sorry. I had no idea," he sighed. We continued our walk. Then David spoke again.

"Kimberly, I believe that things happen for a reason. I know you've had problems in the past, but that doesn't mean we can't step out on faith. Even if we adopt, I would love for us to have a family of our own."

CHAPTER 9

# ROLLER COASTER

Since David was a physician, he'd come across some of the best in Atlanta. He told me about a doctor friend of his, Dr. Cohen. She was a reproductive endocrinologist who had made a name for herself.

So, I reluctantly made the appointment. The office suggested I order my records from my previous doctors and have them with me before I arrived.

The morning of the appointment, I was nervous. I wasn't 100 percent on board and considered canceling. But I loved my husband, and I wanted to be a good wife. I had no expectations that anything would come of this meeting. I was just glad that he was open to adoption, and to me, that was our best and only way to start our family.

Once we arrived, we went through the regular exchange—insurance card, ID, and twenty pages of paperwork. I had my medical records, so a lot of the questions I left blank. While sitting in the lobby, it was hard to make eye contact. Everyone knows you're there because you need "help." Help with something that, to most, is God's greatest gift.

"Mrs. Gowdy?" a small blonde woman called out. David and I both stood and followed her to the back. The plan was for me to have a consultation initially to see how and if we could move forward. I was thirty-nine, which was eighty in fertility years.

She directed us into a small office. Degrees were plastered on much of the walls. I was impressed. No sooner than we got settled, the door swung open.

"Dr. Gowdy, how are you?" greeted a petite, dark-haired woman who was all smiles.

"Dr. Cohen, good to see you." David stood and shook her hand.

"And I assume you are Mrs. Gowdy?" she asked.

"Yes," I said. I could see the manila envelope I'd given the lady at the front desk along with the clipboard. She sat down at the cluttered desk.

"So tell me, what's going on?" I assumed she wanted to know why fertility was our issue. I told her about my previous losses.

"After a few of my pregnancy losses, I had to have a D&C to remove the placenta. The procedure scarred my uterus pretty bad, and the dilation also caused my incompetent cervix, which ended up being my final diagnosis," I explained.

"That is likely the reason for the early effacement," she said. She suggested we take a look at my uterus to get a better idea of how things looked. This type of ultrasound was the worst—that long wand covered with a condom. You almost need to smoke a cigarette after.

She looked intently at the screen, measuring and taking pictures. She printed out a slew of pics, handed me a tissue, and told me to get dressed. We sat in the back waiting room this time. They called me in to give blood. It was the final step before going back in to see Dr. Cohen. I was nervous. These conversations had never been good for me.

"There is some scarring in your uterus," she began. "The good news is that we have a new technique to help reduce scarring. I'll need to perform the procedure laparoscopically," she said. I should have been happy, but I wasn't. "Since you told me you've had so many early-stage miscarriages, I'd like to send a sample of your uterine tissue to Yale University to check for a specific condition that may have affected your previous pregnancies. I'll get the sample if you decide to move forward with the surgery. Lastly, we need to check your fertility age." That part made sense. I was no spring chicken, so I needed to make sure that the procedures were worth moving forward.

David answered before I could even say anything. "Sounds like a plan," he chimed.

They had to measure blood levels at different times, so it required a few trips for either a blood draw or an ultrasound. About a week after the final test, I received a call with the verdict. My fertility age, as she called it, was based on a bunch of hormonal data, my luteal phase, follicle-stimulating hormone (FSH) in my ovaries, and estrogen, and I assume the ultrasounds to make sure I was in sync. According to her, I was thirty-five. Not bad, but not great.

Nonetheless, the doctor scheduled a surgical procedure within the next couple of weeks. Based on her findings, the procedure was a success. The test from Yale took about a month after the surgery, and it turned out there were no problems with my lining either.

It was now time for a protocol. The goal was to get as many viable eggs as possible to create the embryos. The protocols were scientific and based on hormone levels. The gonadotropins cause you to produce an enormous number of eggs in your ovaries until you feel like you're about to burst, then the right amount of propofol sends you into la-la land, the eggs are retrieved, and they use your partner's sperm to create embryos. While I was poked, prodded, clipped, snipped, shot, and anesthetized to retrieve my eggs, David was only asked to go into a room full of dirty magazines and videos to provide his contribution. Funny how that works.

There are three-day transfers and five-day transfers with this procedure. Dr. Cohen suggested we move forward with a five-day transfer, as this meant allowing the embryos to develop for five days to see which ones were viable. Out of all the embryos created, only six made it to five days. Secretly, I was praying it wouldn't work. I'd never had problems with getting pregnant; it was sustaining the pregnancy. The last thing I wanted to do was attempt another pregnancy, but I wanted to be a good wife.

Ten days after the transfer of two five-day blastocysts, the pregnancy test was negative. Although I hadn't wanted to go down this road again, I cried when I got the call. The feeling of failure gripped me all over again. Over the past couple of years, I'd learned to be content regardless of my circumstance, but this wasn't easy.

*Why did I allow myself to go down this road?* I thought. David had already started talking to me about the next attempt, but I couldn't do it. He needed to understand that marriage is a partnership. In my past, I sacrificed my heart, my body, and my finances all under the "good wife" umbrella. No more. Being a good partner doesn't mean sacrificing everything; it doesn't mean forsaking all for the happiness of someone else.

The conversation was not what he wanted to hear, but I was slipping back into a state of depression, and I was trying to hold on to my last bit of sanity. We were told early on that frozen embryos could be donated, so I was willing to make this sacrifice rather than have them destroyed.

David's final response was, "Let's wait and see how you feel a few months from now."

## CHAPTER 10

# WHAT WE DO FOR LOVE

A few months had passed since the transfer of two of our embryos. David and I decided we needed to take a break. Between the surgeries, tests, retrievals, transfers, and negative pregnancy tests, we'd spent close to a year of our lives on high alert. It was time to relax and unwind.

So, we decided to go back to his roots. We traveled back to Montego Bay, Jamaica. Our resort was beautiful. It was secluded and offered the full couple's experience. We also had a chance to visit with his family and enjoy some traditional Jamaican fare—callaloo, jerk chicken, and rice and peas, all washed down with real coconut water, directly from the tree. The trip was just what we needed. We celebrated our anniversary and birthdays all in one vacation. We knew we still wanted a family, but I had my heart set on adoption. His heart, however, wasn't so inclined.

On our last evening in Jamaica, while sitting poolside, I decided to broach the topic.

"So, what are your thoughts about adoption?" I asked.

"I have nothing against adoption. But I'd like us to exhaust this option," David sighed.

"What is this option?" My temper was rising.

"Transferring the rest of our embryos," he said.

"Are you kidding me?" I'd had it at this point. "I told you over a year ago all that I'd gone through, and you still talked me into seeing Dr. Cohen. I had to relive everything all over again!" I was screaming at the top of my lungs. "I'm forty years old. I don't want to keep putting myself through this kind of pain. I've had it!"

I jumped up and went back to the room. About ten minutes later, David came into the room. I was sitting out on the balcony. He slid the glass door open.

"Soooooo, are you mad at me?" I was silent. "I'm sorry. I don't think I realized what a sacrifice you were making for me," he said. He reached for my hand and held me for what seemed like an eternity. "I love you," he said.

"I love you too," I cried.

Once we returned to Atlanta, I contacted Dr. Cohen's office. I had a follow-up appointment with her to consider moving forward with another transfer. I spoke with her nurse to inform them that we were considering adoption. I wanted to know if there was someone they recommended. They immediately gave me the contact information for Attorney Shay Jackson.

We'd been paying everything out of pocket, so the costs were adding up. When we pulled up to the office, we knew right out of the gate this attorney wasn't going to be cheap. The location of the office was in the heart of Buckhead. I guess it's the price you pay for the best. We walked into the beautifully decorated foyer.

A young man in a navy-blue suit greeted us. "Hello, I'm Michael," he said.

"Dr. Gowdy."

"Kimberly Gowdy." We shook hands.

"Can I get you any coffee, water?"

"Water is fine," I said. David nodded his head. Michael directed us into a good-sized conference room. There was a large cherry-wood table, surrounded by ten black chairs trimmed in matching cherry wood.

"I wonder how much all this is going to cost," David said sarcastically.

Michael returned with our waters. "Miss Jackson will be in shortly."

After about five minutes, a woman also wearing a navy suit

greeted us. She had an athletic build and an extremely chiseled face as if she didn't miss a day at the gym.

"Hello, Dr. Gowdy, Mrs. Gowdy. I'm Shay Jackson." She was so matter of fact, I was waiting for her to say, "Miss Jackson if you're nasty."

We had taken seats in the middle of the table. She sat directly in front of us on the opposite side. Michael ran into the room just as we were about to begin. He quickly apologized after she gave him a side-eye.

"So, tell me a little about yourselves," she said. I led the discussion, as David didn't seem to have much to say. "How long have you been considering adoption?" she finally asked, directing her question to David.

"To be perfectly honest, my goal is to raise a family with my wife. I wanted us to share children of our own, but as my wife just expressed, it's now physically impossible."

"You've come to the right place," she said. "I've handled several adoptions, but one thing I heard you mention was that you have frozen embryos."

"Yes, we have four, but there's a service that will allow us to donate our embryos to a loving couple willing to adopt them. I've already looked into it." I was maybe a little too matter of fact.

"No need to be defensive, Mrs. Gowdy. I'm not here to pass judgment, but I do think I may have an option that may make both of you happy. Have you considered surrogacy?" she asked.

"Surrogacy?" David was suddenly sitting up in his chair. "You know, we hadn't thought about that option."

"Well, it would allow you to have a biological child without risking the health of your wife."

"So, what's the process?" David was thirsty for more information. Now I was the disinterested one. The thought of another woman carrying my child put an even greater spotlight on my inadequacies. How could he even think that I would be on board with something like this? I've never known anyone who'd done such a thing. As I sat there watching my husband basking in the opportunity of a stranger spending every minute of every day with my child, I was getting sick. I couldn't bear the thought. I felt like I wanted to jump up from the table and run like Forrest Gump. Hadn't I endured enough?

## CHAPTER 11

# THE DECISION

I left Attorney Jackson's office with more questions than answers. Surrogacy? Does anybody other than celebrities even do this?

The beginning of the drive home with David was nerve-wracking. He went on and on about this being the perfect solution.

"Babe, just look how God has worked this out!" He was excited.

"Let's take some time to think about it," I suggested.

"Think about it? What's there to think about? It's the perfect solution!"

"How does surrogacy even work?" I asked. I had been too embarrassed to say anything in front of Attorney Jackson. I didn't want to sound stupid.

"How does it work as far as what?" David was confused by my question.

"Well, does she have any rights to the baby? What if she doesn't want to give the baby up? Remember that movie we saw on TV?"

"This is our biological child. She has no claims to him or her," he stressed. "Didn't you hear what Attorney Jackson said?" *Actually, no, because I shut down after the word surrogate was said.*

"Remember how excited I was about adoption, but you weren't there yet?" I spoke as softly as I could.

"Yeah," he said.

"Just give me a minute to absorb this new option," I said. "See, with adoption, I can instantly become a mom and enjoy all the benefits of sharing my love with a child who needs me as much as I need them. But with surrogacy, I'll have to be much stronger. I'll endure the day-to-day, week-to-week, month-to-month vision of another woman carrying my child. It will remind me of how easy it is for someone to bring a life into this world, and I'll have to be ready for the questions that may arise. Everyone has an area of their lives where they feel inadequate, and I can't think there would be anyone who would want to be reminded of it daily for almost a year." After my commentary on the subject, David reached for my hand and held it for the rest of the ride home.

I had been doing some serious praying and reflecting. I guess this all boiled down to how badly I wanted to be a mom. How bad the joy of raising my child outweighed my feelings of inadequacy. Lord knows that over the years, there were times when this feeling was more prevalent.

I was the eldest of eight—seven girls and a boy—so I was Aunt Kimberly to about twelve children. Not counting my sorority sisters' children. I was still close to all my siblings and a number of my sorors, so of course, they wanted me to share in their joy.

Over the past ten-plus years, "Congratulations! Oh, what a beautiful baby!" had become my number-one line. To my credit, with each of those calls and baby showers, I never let my pain overshadow their joy. I believe it's about being genuinely happy for others and knowing that your time will come.

I had some close friends who would say what I wanted to hear, but I needed a friend who would tell me the truth. I made a phone call to Wisconsin; I knew Sherry always had a word for me.

"OOP-SKEE," she signaled when she answered.

"SKEE-OOP," I replied heartily. That was always how we started our conversations in honor of our sororities.

"Hey girl, how you doin'?" Sherry was a down-to-earth sistah; I loved that about her.

"I'm struggling with a decision about surrogacy," I admitted. I told Sherry about our meeting with Attorney Jackson and how I was feeling.

"Is raising a child important to you?" she asked.

"Of course!" I thought that was an odd question.

"Will using a surrogate better your chances of making that happen?"

"Well, yes," I replied.

"Then, that's your answer."

"I'm just concerned about the appearance, needing to use someone else to carry my child."

Sherry sighed. "If you needed a heart transplant, would you accept someone's heart?" she asked.

"Of course, in a heartbeat! Get it? Heartbeat?" I laughed at my own joke.

"That was corny, but like I was saying, people give of themselves all the time, from kidneys to livers to eyes, and in this case, a uterus. How is it any different?" she asked.

"Hmmm, message received," I sighed.

We laughed and talked about so many other things, and the call ended on a high note. For the first time in days, I was feeling good about this possibility. As fate would have it, my sister Courtney called. She had been thinking about me. I shared how I was battling with this decision, and this thought of *What if my child asks me how I felt when I carried him?*

"I don't know that any of my children have ever asked me that," she laughed. "But if they did, you can tell them their story and tell them how much they were wanted and loved. It's no different than if you had adopted them." I was now 100 percent sure what I wanted to do at this point.

I invited David to meet me for dinner at a local seafood restaurant after work. It had been almost a month since we met with Attorney Jackson. He'd stopped talking about the possibility of surrogacy. I think he figured I hadn't warmed to the idea.

"Gowdy, party of two," the server dressed in all black shouted. David and I stood, and he placed his hand on my lower back, motioning me to walk in front of him. We ordered a bottle of cabernet and the Alpharetta Roll.

"Glad you could make it," I started the conversation.

"How else would I eat?"

"Insinuating that I didn't cook?" We laughed, but he did have a point. "I've been thinking a lot about our decision to use a surrogate," I said, but then David interrupted.

"Wait, before you go any further, I've been thinking too. I've decided that our life is fine the way it is."

"But I want to use a surrogate," I blurted out.

"What?" He looked surprised.

"I think we should do it. I think I'll be okay." I was starting to get excited about going through the process. I hadn't seen this smile on my husband's face since we said "I do" for the first time in the pastor's office.

For the next two hours we talked, toasted, and laughed. We were about to embark on the journey of a lifetime.

We met with Attorney Jackson to go over the next steps and sign on the dotted line. She would be handling background checks and any other legalities that presented themselves in this process.

"You'll be referred to from now on as intended parents, or IPs," she said.

"How do we go about finding a surrogate?" David asked.

"I have a few agencies in mind," Attorney Jackson said. "Some of our clients have used them. I'm considering adding this service to my practice, but I'm not quite there yet. Quite frankly, we're finding that some IPs are finding surrogates on the internet. But regardless of how you find your surrogate, remember you are looking for a gestational surrogate; she is someone who will have no biological ties to your child. She is merely the oven."

After the meeting with Attorney Jackson, we contacted Dr. Cohen's office and told her about our decision.

"I think you're making a sound decision," she said. She thought this was the best option considering my history. She informed us that the finance team would discuss financial packages that could help to keep our costs low once we made it to this step so that, instead of costing an arm and a leg, it might just be the leg.

"The first thing you need to do is contact a psychologist. I've had great success with Dr. Whaley over in the Perimeter," she advised.

"Is this mandatory?" David asked.

"It is for our clinic. You're embarking on a big step, an expensive step. Although I can uncover any physical concerns, the last thing you want to do is go further down the road, then find out your surrogate has some psychological challenges." The process made perfect sense.

The world of surrogacy is vast, but agencies can lessen your load. They have proven vetted surrogates who are assessable for a fee. The cost for most was an upfront five thousand dollars. I'd originally thought this was much too expensive, as success is not guaranteed.

I chose the internet route. In hindsight, if I had to do it again, I would have chosen an agency.

I read hundreds of posts from different surrogates as I searched for the perfect match. Lots of women placed ads offering to help other women build their families. I scoured these sites for weeks. All I knew was that I wanted an African American surrogate. In my mind, I believed I could live vicariously through this woman, and if so, it would be much easier if she were black like me.

## CHAPTER 12

# STRIKE 1, 2, 3!

After months of searching, I finally found someone who seemed to be the ideal candidate. She had children, and from her picture, she looked to be in great physical shape. As a plus, she was available to get started immediately.

I took down her contact information and emailed her that same day. I was delighted that I received an immediate response. She gave me her phone number and asked me to call at my earliest convenience. My earliest convenience was now. I nervously dialed the number.

"Hello," a cheerful voice answered.

"Hello, may I speak with Alisa?"

"Speaking."

"Hi, Alisa. This is Kimberly. I'm the one who emailed you about possibly becoming a surrogate." I was hoping I didn't sound too anxious.

"Yes, I've wanted to do this for a while," she said.

"So, have you done this before?" I wasn't sure what to ask, but I thought that was appropriate.

"No, this would be my first time, but again, it's something that I've always wanted to do."

"I see you live in Tucker. Maybe we could set up a day to meet?"

"That would be great," she said with enthusiasm.

"Did my number show up on your caller ID?" I asked, but I knew it hadn't. I'd dialed *67 to block my number just in case things didn't go well.

"No, it actually shows that it's restricted."

I gave her my phone number and let her know I'd be contacting her to coordinate the meeting with her, my husband, and I.

I gave David the rundown about the call. Just as I expected, he was ecstatic. I reached back out to Alisa, and we made plans to meet for breakfast at a local chain restaurant. We gave her our physical descriptions and told her the color and make of our car. She did the same.

The initial meeting felt somewhat like meeting someone you might meet from online dating. It can be a little awkward at first, but if it's the right one, things can move forward pretty quickly.

As David and I sat in the car, we noticed a tall, curvaceous African American female with a short bob exiting her car. Both she and the car fit her description, but I added in the curvaceous feature. I assumed it was her. I opened my door and called out.

"Alisa?" Her head turned quickly. I waved and said, "It's me, Kimberly." She gave a kind smile and started walking in my direction.

By then, David was exiting the car. She looked over at him and gave the same kind smile.

"It's so nice to meet you." I beamed. I was a little nervous. After we exchanged pleasantries, we made our way into the restaurant. Luckily, since it was a weekday, the place wasn't crowded. We were seated in a booth close to the back.

"So, are you married?" was David's first question.

"No, I'm divorced," she replied.

"How many children do you have?"

"Two," she answered. After about one hundred and one questions from us, we asked her if she had any questions for us. "So why are you choosing to use a surrogate?" Her question made perfect sense. I gave a high-level overview of our struggles. She seemed to empathize, and her compassion was a good sign. She asked a few more questions, but all in all, it was a great first meeting.

We all decided to set up a time for David and I to go to her home and meet her children. We wanted to see where our little munchkin could be cohabitating for nine months.

About a week after meeting Alisa, we made a trip to her home. It was quaint with lots of character. She introduced us to her two children, Jaden and Ke'sha. From the looks of them, she'd done a great job. She showed us around her home. We even played a while with her children.

"We would love to move forward with you as our surrogate," I said.

"I was hoping you'd say that. I'd love to do it." Alisa smiled. It was official. We told her the next steps as we understood it. David and I would meet alone with the psychologist, Dr. Whaley, first.

Our first appointment was scheduled in the middle of the day with Dr. Whaley in the Perimeter. We entered the building and walked down a long hallway. We came to a door with a metal nameplate bearing her name. Upon walking in, an older white woman with short blonde hair looked up at us.

"Gowdys, I presume?" she asked with a warm voice.

"Yes," we said in unison.

"Have a seat right over here." Her office looked like a living room set with two loveseats, end tables, and modern lamps, one on each end of the loveseats. We sat on the loveseats; she sat with her legs crossed in a beautiful high-back wing chair directly in front of us.

"It's so good to meet you," she said.

"Same," David replied.

"Thank you for sending over your information ahead of time. It always helps to have information before the meeting," she stressed.

"It's been quite a journey. Hopefully, this session will go as planned," I said.

"Could you tell me the name of the potential surrogate?"

"Yes, her name is Alisa Brown." I was excited.

"The way we would proceed is, I will meet with the two of

you first, then I'll meet the potential surrogate and her partner, if applicable, and finally, I'll meet with all parties," Dr. Whaley explained.

"So, Dr. Cohen and Attorney Jackson are required to sign off before we can move forward?" asked David.

"Correct. And I'm glad you're working with Dr. Cohen. She and I work pretty well together." She smiled.

"So, tell me a little bit about your surrogate." I gave her as much information as I could and explained that we'd only met twice, but we'd spoken quite a bit over the phone.

"With all potential surrogates, I have them take an MMPI," Dr. Whaley said. "It's a psych evaluation, about five hundred questions, and it's pretty intense. Alisa and I would meet more than once. The cost is all out of pocket to you, of course." We nodded.

After delving deeper into the minds of David and me, she asked us to have our surrogate reach out to her, and they would schedule their visits. The appointment seemed to go well.

About a week later, I received a call that changed everything.

"Hello," I answered.

"Hello, Kimberly, this is Dr. Whaley." She didn't sound very upbeat.

"Hi, is everything okay?" I asked.

"Well, not really. It's about your surrogate. I spoke with Alisa and found out she'd previously taken the MMPI," she said. That was surprising. She'd never even mentioned it. "Unfortunately, I won't be able to recommend her."

I was confused. "She's already taken the MMPI," I said.

"Yes, she'd previously taken it, but the results were borderline. Also, before I received her test results, my notes state that she attended a gathering with the previous IPs and ended up in a compromising position with one of the guests. That, coupled with the results of the test, meant I couldn't recommend her. Without my recommendation, we can't move forward."

"But we got our hopes up," I said.

"I'm afraid my position won't change," she said. I was disappointed. I phoned Alisa right after.

"Hi Alisa," I sighed.

"I can already tell you must have spoken with Dr. Whaley," she said.

"Yes, I did. Why didn't you say anything?" I asked.

"It was over a year ago, so I didn't think it mattered. I'm so sorry." We ended the call, and I never spoke to her again after that.

Although I was disappointed with how things ended with Alisa, I knew I needed to continue moving forward. I was determined. I'd previously set up an email account to use specifically for my correspondence with potential surrogates. Over the past several months, I'd received some emails from women who were interested in speaking to me. Most of them were in other states, so I didn't even consider them, but I was getting desperate. It was time for desperate measures.

As I scrolled down my emails, one email jumped out at me. *I THINK I CAN HELP YOU*. I'd seen this email before, and I remembered the surrogate was in Florida. That wouldn't be so bad. I could hop on a plane and be in Florida in no time.

I decided to email her. *Hi Taylor, I hope you are well. I want to discuss the possibility of working with you as a surrogate.*

Three days later, I received an email from Taylor. The email listed her phone number and the best time to call. Her email read that evenings after eight o'clock were the best time. I think we called her at 8:01.

"Hello," a friendly voice answered.

"Hello, may I speak with Taylor?" I kindly asked.

"Speaking." I introduced myself and asked her if she was still interested in becoming a surrogate. The answer was yes.

"I'm going to put you on speaker, is that okay? My husband, David, is here, and I would love for him to join the conversation," I said.

"That would be fine. My husband is sitting here as well, so I'll put you on speaker too."

"Hi, Taylor, this is David." He uses David when he wants to sound informal. Taylor's husband was named Eric. He was very talkative, which was good, so he kept the conversation going.

Taylor had already taken the MMPI, so we were good on that front. But even better than that, she had already been a successful surrogate for another couple. That was music to our ears.

We spoke with Attorney Jackson the very next day. We wanted to move fast. Since Taylor was out of state, there were childcare expenses for her two children and the cost of travel and lodging to and from Atlanta, including meals. We knew we were all in at this point, so we were prepared to foot the bill. I spoke with Taylor just about every day. She was very close to her family, so there'd be times when I got a chance to meet her extended family over the phone.

Things were coming together nicely. Dr. Cohen wanted to see Taylor within a certain window of her cycle, so we purchased the plane tickets accordingly. We'd gotten pretty comfortable with Taylor and Eric, so we extended an invitation for them to stay at our home for this trip. Besides, it did save us a little extra cash.

The drive to the airport brought on a lot of anxiety. I wanted to drive. I needed to keep my mind on something other than my nerves. We'd seen countless pictures of Taylor and her family at this point, so recognizing them wouldn't be a problem. Then, the phone rang.

"Hello Taylor," I answered right away. I recognized her number.

"Hi Kimberly, we are outside of baggage claim. There's an N5 on the door."

"That's perfect. Just look for a silver sedan. We are driving up now." My heart was pounding.

"I have on a red jacket, braided hair in a high ponytail . . . wait, I think I see you." We saw someone waving their hand, and the bright-red jacket was a giveaway. I had to double-park alongside another car. We both jumped out of the car, and the hugs ensued.

"It's so good to meet you finally," I said. Taylor shared the same sentiment. We were oblivious to the cars honking at us until Atlanta's Finest gave us the side-eye.

"Let's keep it moving, folks," a heavy-set black officer directed. We hopped in the car and made our way back to Alpharetta.

"So, are you guys hungry?" David asked.

"Actually, yes. The snack on the plane did nothing."

"What do you have a taste for?" I asked.

"We eat anything," Taylor announced.

I followed up with, "Well, my favorite food is Mexican. I've never met a chimichanga that I didn't like." We all laughed and agreed to go to a local Mexican restaurant in Alpharetta.

During dinner, the conversation was easy. We enjoyed this couple, and we were so glad that we decided to move forward.

Taylor and Eric would be spending two days in Atlanta. We had an appointment to see the psychologist, Dr. Whaley, first. We were sure she would clear us, especially since we'd already jumped the MMPI hurdle. The following day would be the physical exam, and we were sure that would also go well.

Dr. Whaley met with Taylor and Eric for about an hour before calling David and me into her office. Just as expected, Dr. Whaley's report was glowing. She felt we had the right chemistry and that we'd get through the process just fine.

The following day would be the biggest and most expensive. We'd taken Dr. Cohen up on her IVF package to help with expenses. We knew what we were getting into and were committed.

David and I waited in a private waiting area for Taylor to go through the examination. When the nurse finally came out to get us, it felt like it had been hours when, in actuality, it had only been about forty-five minutes. She ushered us into Dr. Cohen's cluttered office. She was sitting behind her desk.

"I'm concerned about Taylor's weight," she blurted out. "I had a heart-to-heart talk with Taylor about this. My recommendation is that she loses at least twenty-five pounds before we move forward." I was speechless.

"Other than her weight, how was everything else?" David asked.

"Her vitals were fine, and her uterus and ovaries all look perfectly normal. We took blood, but we won't know those levels for a day or two."

"If we decide we still want to move forward, would you honor that?" I was getting teary-eyed.

"Kimberly, the embryos are yours. It's your money, and I can't say for certain that she won't be fine carrying your child, so I'm not totally against it. It's just that I have concerns."

We continued our discussion with Dr. Cohen, and her concerns made sense, but after getting this far I wasn't going to give up without uncovering every possibility. We finally came to a unanimous decision.

The three of us entered a small waiting room just down the hall. Eric and Taylor were sitting at the round table. I looked Taylor in the eyes.

"Everything is fine," I assured her. "We're going to be moving forward."

As we all spoke with Dr. Cohen, her concerns seemed to diminish in my eyes, likely because she could see the desperation on my face. In the end, it was our decision. Taylor was our choice, and we were going for it.

Based on the lab results, a protocol was determined. Since Taylor lived out of state, we would have the medications delivered to her home—estrogen and progesterone to thicken up her lining, making it ready for our embryos. We made arrangements to have Taylor monitored in Florida. Once her lining measured to perfection, we would have her and Eric flown back for the transfer.

A little over two months later, the time for the transfer came, and we were back at the airport. That morning, David and I were on pins and needles. Taylor was fine, and she'd been through the process before, so she was way ahead of us in the knowledge department.

We sat in the main waiting area at the doctor's office. "Taylor," the nurse called in the room. Taylor and Eric both stood. "Dr. and Mrs. Gowdy, you can come as well," she smiled.

Taylor was asked to go into a separate room, and Eric followed. David and I had prayed so much before this, but there was always room for one more. We prayed that all would be blessed and that we would receive the desires of our hearts.

The door finally opened. "Dr. and Mrs. Gowdy," she called, and she directed us into a dimly lit room. Dr. Cohen was already standing there with a face mask on, gown, and gloves. Taylor was lying on the table in stirrups, Eric at her side. There was also another doctor in the room. We found out he was the embryologist.

"Hello, I'm Dr. Singh. Pleased to meet you," he greeted. He directed us to look at a large screen with what looked like four blobs. We knew from our attempt at in vitro fertilization, or IVF, that they were all five-day blastocysts. We had to decide, with his help, how many and which one(s) we wanted to use.

He had already graded them and had pretty much decided for us. We decided to concede to his knowledge, as we didn't know. Ultimately, he decided on two. David and I stood on the side opposite Eric. She had a sheet draped over her lower half. After the speculum was inserted, it was show time.

You could hear a pin drop. The four of us watched as the embryologist succinctly and carefully handed off our embryos to Dr. Cohen.

"Keep your eyes on the ultrasound machine," she said. We watched as the catheter made its way into Taylor's womb. I thought I'd be in tears, but at that moment, I was full of anticipation. I was sure this was it. I was on my way to becoming a mom.

Now was the time to wait. Taylor and Eric headed home. Dr. Cohen told us the blood work would be performed in ten days;

she'd already sent the order to the RE in Florida. In the world of IVF, ten days seemed like a lifetime, so Taylor and I agreed to use our own test.

Instead of relying solely on the ten-day blood test, we decided to use the five-day pee test. I'd purchased five EPT tests at the local pharmacy and gave them to Taylor. She would update me after each early-morning pee. We were hardly the only ones taking this route. I'd gone online to IVF sites and seen some women who had positive 5dpt after 5dpt, which in layman's terms means positive pregnancy test, five days after the transfer of a five-day embryo. Even a faint line or a faint plus sign would give me hope. Of course, the possibility of seeing neither never crossed my mind.

We were on day ten. I should have been excited, but I was dreading the call from Dr. Cohen. Every test that Taylor had taken was negative. The chance there would be a different outcome was highly unlikely. I was on my way to the office when I got the call.

"Good morning, Kimberly. I wish I had better news for you," she said. Where had I heard that before?

"How soon can we try again?" I asked.

"Well, that depends. You wouldn't be using the same surrogate, right?"

"Well, I thought we could try with Taylor again."

"The only way I would be willing to move forward with her is if she loses at least twenty-five pounds," she said emphatically. As much as I wanted to go against Dr. Cohen, her intuition so far had been right. I expressed Dr. Cohen's concerns to Taylor and Eric. They understood completely. Taylor asked that we allow her a chance to lose the weight. She was committed to our goal, and at this point, I was happy to have her on our journey.

David and I needed some time away from the process. While Taylor worked toward her BMI goal, we decided we needed some TLC. We agreed to reconvene in about six months in hopes that taking a step back would allow a better outcome. David and

I enjoyed the summer, enjoyed time with family in the fall, and rang in the new year with great expectations.

I'd had some calls with Taylor, checking in on her progress. She seemed to be doing well. An appointment was set up for Taylor in Florida, full physical including blood work. Dr. Cohen called me with the news.

"Hello, Kimberly."

"Hello, Dr. Cohen," I answered. I was ready to get back in the saddle.

"Kimberly, we cannot move forward with Taylor."

"Why not? You told me she needed to lose weight, and she's lost weight." I was furious.

"Kimberly, not only has she not lost the weight, but her A1C level is prediabetic. Ethically, I cannot move forward with Taylor."

There wasn't much I could say to Taylor other than to express my disappointment. At this point, I wanted off this roller-coaster ride.

It had now been well over a year since we found the first surrogate. I had started expressing my apprehension to David. "I don't know how much longer I can do this!" I shouted.

"Let's just give it some more time."

"Time? Are you kidding me? Exactly how much 'time' are you putting into this? All you have to do is show up. I'm the one taking the time to make these connections in the first place!" I yelled.

"You're right, I'm sorry," he said, walking over to me. "Let's agree to give this one more shot. If it doesn't work, we can look into adoption, okay?" He held me close. He knew that between my career and the heaviness of blaming myself for our infertility struggles, this was becoming too much.

I'd waited close to four months before I started looking again, but I managed to reach out to yet another potential surrogate, Latoya. Latoya lived in Atlanta, married with one child. On paper, things looked perfect, but I remained guarded. I explained to her that our last potential surrogate had a few unexpected medical issues.

"No one has ever diagnosed me with any medical issues," was her response. We decided to meet at Centennial Park; it would be a nice way to get to know each other. The meeting went well. Shortly after that, we were back in Dr. Whaley's office. She met with them and then all of us as a group. Latoya passed the MMPI.

It was time for the moment of truth—the physical exam. David and I were on pins and needles.

"Dr. and Mrs. Gowdy," a young nurse called into the waiting room. She directed David and me into Dr. Cohen's cluttered office. We saw her sitting behind her huge, paper-covered desk.

"Have a seat, you two. What are the odds?" We were confused by her question. "Latoya is a lovely woman, but there could be a problem." At that moment, I slinked down in my chair in an exaggerated "here we go again" posture.

Dr. Cohen continued. "We found a fibroid, not huge, but big enough, that we would recommend surgery before we get started. You'd still have to wait for her to recover from that surgery as well, so you might be looking at the end of the year before we could proceed.

"I'm sorry," she said. She could see the pain on my face. At that point, I was officially done!

## CHAPTER 13

# NOT AGAIN

The sting of the past three years hit us pretty hard. Three surrogates had ended badly, not to mention the countless conversations with women who didn't even make it to the first face-to-face. David and I needed time to regain our bearings and get refocused. We had put all our eggs in one basket, literally.

As I said, when I agreed to marry David, I was under the impression that it would be just the two of us. I was ready to embrace my bonus mom role with David's daughters, Angela and Gabrielle, and even an occasional family outing with his ex-wife, Diana. But the thought of bringing another full-time person into our world had never entered the equation. We had between twelve and fifteen nieces and nephews and counting, plus two grandchildren at this point. We had more than enough children to love.

I knew what I brought to the marriage. I brought the ability to love, the desire to be loved, laughter, financial stability, and warmth on a cool Atlanta night. But I also knew my limitations, and one of them was infertility. I'd worked my way up to a salary well into the six figures, a salary that still didn't compare to David's. That alone offered us a chance to live our lives without limits.

Without the expense of children, we could enjoy our lives in other ways. David and I were both frugal. We still lived in our same subdivision, the one he'd told me about years ago, and once we got married, he sold his place and moved into mine. I was still driving my eleven-year-old sedan. But wasn't it time to stretch out? Bask in our success? Purchase the home of our dreams? I could finally get my dream car and vacation in some of the most beautiful places the world has to offer.

For the next few years, we didn't speak of adoption or surrogacy. We were enjoying life. The only time we thought about our surrogacy was when we received a bill for the storage of our embryos. We had a chance to witness an historic presidential election and participate in all the theater that surrounded it. I think David even got a little bit of the political fever. More to come on that.

Back when we were still going through the surrogacy process, David and I had both accepted new positions, his in Tifton, Georgia, and mine near the Perimeter off of Highway 285. I was now working from home 90 percent of the time. My new job was a blessing. Not only did it enrich me financially, but it also allowed me to travel back and forth to Tifton with David. We still officially lived three hundred miles away in Alpharetta, but we lived two weeks in Tifton and two weeks in Alpharetta. Every two weeks, we packed up and drove for three hours to and from Tifton. The good news was that, in Tifton, David could leave our apartment at 7:50 and be at the hospital with a cup of coffee by eight.

One day, I received a call from David. There was a young woman in the hospital who was considering giving up her baby for adoption. David had previously shared our journey with some of the hospital staff, and they wanted to help.

David and I found ourselves happy about the possibility. I thought we'd gotten past these feelings. Hadn't we moved past the desire to raise a child together? The answer was no.

Ultimately, the young woman decided to keep her child, and we prayed that she'd made the right decision, but this momentary encounter had awakened a desire that neither of us knew still existed. We still wanted a child.

We decided we wanted an older child, a son. We would train

him up in the way that he should go, and he would be the perfect addition for his two much older siblings.

The truth for David and me was that no trip, house, or fancy car could compare to the love of a child. Whatever the desire of your heart, there can be no substitute.

It was hard to believe that I was about to make a call to Attorney Jackson. I must have been a glutton for punishment. Or a woman who was living in complete denial about wanting to become a mom.

"Jackson and Associates," a familiar voice answered.

"Hello, Michael?" I guessed.

"Uh, yes. How can I help you?" He seemed confused at my familiarity.

"It's Kimberly Gowdy; I don't know if you remem—"

"Miss Gowdy!" he interrupted. "Of course I remember you. How have you been?" he asked.

"I'm doing well," I answered.

"And your husband?"

"He's doing great too."

"So, how can I help?" He sounded genuinely excited.

"Well, David and I are still considering adoption. We should have done this a long time ago, but everything happens for a reason."

"It certainly does," he agreed. "Attorney Jackson is actually with another couple right now, but I can have her call you."

"That would be great."

"You know, we've changed our services," he said. "We've added surrogacy, and we're vetting our own candidates. It's something Attorney Jackson has talked about for a long time," he whispered.

"I vaguely remember that she was moving in that direction," I sighed.

"I'll have her give you a call ASAP," Michael said.

"Thank you so much, Michael."

"My pleasure."

I felt good after the call. I'd made the first step.

At the time, David had expressed interest in becoming a delegate for the Sixth District of Georgia. We'd been so involved in the previous election that I guess it energized him. He had about two months to get his speech together. The elections would take place in April 2012, and between our work travel and work itself, we didn't have a lot of time. He'd also expressed interest in living full time in Alpharetta. Tifton had some of the nicest people, but the commute was wearing on us.

I was helping prepare his delegate speech when the phone rang. It was Attorney Jackson.

"Hello, Attorney Jackson," I immediately said.

"Kimberly, how are you? When Michael gave me your message, I couldn't wait to call back."

I put the call on speaker. "Hello, Attorney Jackson," David shouted. We exchanged pleasantries and got down to the nature of our call. I talked to her about our close call with the young woman in Tifton and how it got us to thinking about raising a child together. She seemed thrilled.

"Kimberly, tell me, did you guys ever move forward with a surrogate?" she asked.

"Of course not," I said. "We would have called you. Who else would have written the contract?"

"I was hoping you'd say that, but I just wanted to check. I still have the paperwork we started for the embryo donation. What did you ever decide to do?"

"Believe it or not, we're still paying the storage. We just haven't been focused on that." I was starting to feel guilty.

"Michael told me why you called, and I think I have the perfect solution for you." I was suddenly thrilled. "As it turns out, almost all of what I do is surrogacy." She lost me at surrogacy, but I still listened. "I have the perfect person for the two of you." She sounded so sure of herself.

"Perfect person for what?" I wanted to be clear. "I called about adoption, and I hope you're not talking about surrogacy." I raised my voice for emphasis.

"Well, okay, but I just wanted to run this by you. I can understand if you're apprehensive, but please hear me out. Let me start by saying that, outside of your doctor, as your attorney, I know better than just about anybody what you've been through. I know you haven't had much success going the surrogacy route, but—"

"Wait," I interrupted before she could even finish. "I just want to be clear. You're not talking to us about moving forward with another surrogate, right?"

"In all honesty, yes."

"Oh, no, no, no, no. You know what? I can't have this conversation," I said. At that point, David stood.

"Kimberly, just let her finish," he said quietly while gently touching my hand. "We all know, especially Attorney Jackson, what we've endured, so I don't think she would do anything or say anything that would cause us harm, so let's hear her out." He nodded his head to get my agreement. I rolled my eyes and continued to shake my head in disbelief that they would even be entertaining this conversation.

"Go ahead, Attorney Jackson," David directed.

"I have a person who I believe would be an amazing surrogate," Attorney Jackson continued. "She was working with my agency with another couple. However, their personalities didn't click. Did I say she's amazing? She's local, and the best news is that she's been a surrogate before, and she can start right away. She's already taken the MMPI, and her husband's name is also David."

I glanced over at David. I studied his face through squinted eyes; I could see the elation on his face. I couldn't believe how quickly he'd moved from the possibility of adopting to going back down the previous road of heartache and turmoil.

"Attorney Jackson, thank you, but no thank you," I cut in angrily. "This sounds great, but frankly, my heart can't take any more."

"But she—" she continued.

"Please!" I screamed. "We don't want to do this." David

rubbed his head with both hands, then pulled his hand over his face. His body language signaled that I wasn't speaking for him.

"Kimberly, we have two more embryos left," he said. "It might be worth a try." I was in disbelief. "Maybe we could at least meet her, just to see what type of vibe we get. If we don't like her, we can just walk away."

David looked excited. Now I was the one rubbing my head and face and wringing my hands together. I looked like I was ready for the psych ward.

"Okay, okay! We'll meet her," I blurted. I could swear I heard a squeal come from the phone.

"Did I tell you she was local and could start right way?" Now she was repeating herself. "She's married too."

"I bet her husband's name is David," I chimed in sarcastically.

"She's in great physical shape as well," she continued excitedly. She went on and on again reiterating that this potential surrogate was local and able to start right away. She and her husband also had two children of their own.

"Okay, okay, we get it. She's great." I couldn't take it anymore.

"When can we come in to meet them?" David asked.

"I'm thinking early next week," Attorney Jackson said. "I'll have Michael call you to set it up." My eyes were almost stuck in my head they were rolled so high.

"I'm so super excited about hearing from Michael." My comment dripped with sarcasm.

"Sounds good," David chimed. "We'll see you next week." Attorney Jackson was silent. "So, we'll see you next week," David said again.

"Oh, I don't know if I mentioned one small detail," she said hesitantly. "Her name is Heidi. Oh, and she's white. Can't wait to see you both next week!" She quickly hung up.

## CHAPTER 14

# OFF TO A GOOD START

I hadn't been able to eat or sleep since the call with Attorney Jackson. David and I had barely said a word to each other, yet we were supposed to show up as a united front to meet with Heidi.

"Are you okay?" David asked.

"Are you kidding me? Heidi's white?! Does she remember what we look like?" I snapped.

"Yes, it will be fine," David said.

"Okay, I can already hear the questions from people," I sighed. "So much for seeing myself vicariously through her. Does she even have a tan?" I said with even more sarcasm. "And she has the nerve to have the name Heidi, which is like the whitest name on the planet." I scowled.

"I think you're too worried about what other people will say," David said. "Look, DNA starts with the sperm and the egg, so this will biologically be our child no matter who carries him or her." David tried to console me, but I just got up and walked out of the room.

Michael had called as planned and set up the appointment. We agreed to meet on March 5 at 4:30 in Attorney Jackson's office. Driving up to this familiar place was where it had all begun. Five years prior, I was there for the first time asking about adoption, but once David heard that magic word, surrogacy, he was hooked. He was hooked then, and he was hooked now. Attorney Jackson had managed to change the course of my life for the second time.

David and I said a prayer before we got out of the car, the most togetherness we'd had in the past four days. I was usually nervous before these meetings, and today was no different. My heart was about to jump out of my chest.

David and I entered Attorney Jackson's office. The foyer was empty.

"Wow, looks like they've done a huge remodel," David said as he took it all in.

"Yep, drapes are my focus right now," I said sarcastically. We looked up and saw Michael cascading down the steps.

"Hey, you two."

"Hello, Michael." I greeted him with a big hug. He and David shook hands.

"Attorney Jackson is in that conference room." He gestured toward the double doors to the left of us. "She's with Heidi and Dave. She had them come thirty minutes early, but they should be finishing up any minute." David took a seat in one of the two black leather high-back office chairs in the foyer. I chose to stand. I couldn't take my eyes off that door.

Suddenly, one of the doors swung open. Attorney Jackson, stood before us looking just as majestic as ever. She was sure to close the door behind her. No peeking.

"Hello, David and Kimberly." We each hugged her. "Are you guys ready?" she asked.

"Ready as ever," was David's response. I shrugged my shoulders. Attorney Jackson walked over to the door and opened it. I walked in first, David on my heels, followed by Attorney Jackson.

The moment I entered the room, Heidi and I locked eyes. I tried to manage a smile. I knew I looked nervous. She and her David—Dave—stood as we walked into the room. I walked over to her and extended my hand. She briefly looked down at my hand, then leaned in and hugged me. I knew Attorney Jackson must have shared our story. It was as if her hug said, "I know." My guard was coming down, and all it took was a hug. I no longer wanted a quick meeting. I suddenly wanted to get to know Heidi and Dave.

After we exchanged greetings, we took our places, sitting directly across from each other. Heidi looked close to what I'd imagined. She had blonde, curly hair, a petite frame, and small freckles that covered her face. Dave had a medium frame, a friendly smile, and bright-red hair. Sitting there together, I thought they belonged on top of a wedding cake.

Attorney Jackson opened the meeting. "I wanted the four of you to meet because I believe in my heart that Heidi could help you start your family. As I stated, she's done this before," she said.

"I'm glad to be here," said Heidi. She gave a big smile. Both Davids nodded their heads in agreement.

"I honestly didn't want to come," I blurted. The room fell silent. "I wanted to adopt. I've already been through the highs and lows of surrogacy, and quite frankly, I wanted no part of this until I walked into this room. I really don't know what it is, but I feel like we were supposed to meet." I started to cry.

Attorney Jackson decided to excuse herself to allow us to get to know each other.

"Heidi, what made you want to become a surrogate?" I thought this was the perfect icebreaker.

"I feel like this is a calling. Being able to help someone in such a special way blesses me." She was emotional.

"Was it hard to let the baby go after your first surrogacy?" I asked.

"Not at all. Giving of myself in this way makes me happy." Her face lit up. We talked about everything from how we met our spouses to their two beautiful children, our careers, and more. The conversation was easy.

It was my David who realized the time. "Hey, would you guys like to grab a bite to eat?" he asked.

"Sounds good," said Heidi.

"Any place in particular?" my David asked.

"No, we don't have a preference."

I couldn't help myself. As if on cue, I said, "Hey, there's a Mexican restaurant around the corner." We all agreed. *I've never met a chimichanga I didn't like*, I thought to myself.

We said our goodbyes to Attorney Jackson, and promised to contact her the following day.

Once we made our way to the restaurant, the conversation continued. It was time to bring out the pictures. Heidi's children were beautiful. She beamed as she showed them off. I was proud to show off my parents, nieces, and siblings.

"I didn't realize you had such a large family and so many sisters." She looked puzzled. I knew what she was thinking. *Why didn't she ask her siblings?*

"When I lost my son, Elijah, I remember receiving a letter from my youngest sister, Asjah. I read her letter through tears as she lamented how painful it was for her to see her sister endure this level of pain, and she offered to carry my child for me. It blessed me beyond measure to know that she would ask to do this for me, but I'm the eldest. I'm the one who puts out fires and stands in the gap for my siblings. It crossed my mind, but the thought was fleeting." I expressed this to Heidi the best way I could.

"Kimberly, while I understand your feelings, there's nothing wrong with asking for help," she said.

"I absolutely agree," I said. "Honestly, before I went through the process with the last three surrogates, I asked Dr. Cohen if reaching out to a friend or family member would make sense. She was dead set against it. Her position was that too many issues could arise during this process that could put a strain on the relationship, like feelings of sibling rivalry and jealousy. For instance, seeing your child with his favorite aunt may bring on different feelings if she also carried him," I explained.

"Wow, I never really thought about it that way," said Heidi. She and I were now in our own world just chatting up a storm.

"Are you ready to order?" our server, Chelsea, asked.

"I'll have the chicken chimi with extra queso on the side and a side of guac, no beans, no rice." That order just freely rolls off my tongue every time.

David and I always pray before we eat, even at a restaurant. But once the food arrived, Heidi's Dave asked, "David, do you want to me to lead the prayer?" That was music to our ears. We wanted someone who believed in the power of prayer. If we decided to take this journey, we would need all the prayer we could get.

It was getting late, so it was time to pack it up.

"Thank you all so much for having dinner with us," said David. He motioned the server for the check.

"I can help take care of the bill," said Heidi's Dave.

"Absolutely not," my David said. "If we can't afford to pay for dinner, we should probably not be contemplating surrogacy." We all laughed, but David was right.

Once we all stood to leave, I lagged behind a little and made light conversation with Heidi.

"So, I would love for you to be our surrogate, that is, if you want to." It felt like I was asking her for a second date. It was a little awkward.

"Let me go home and discuss it with my children," Heidi said. "I will call you tomorrow morning with my decision." That was good enough for me.

The night ended just as it began. Heidi gave me a warm hug, and it was as if she had already answered my question. I believed her answer would be yes.

## CHAPTER 15

# SHE SAID?

David and I talked about Heidi and Dave the entire morning. We were hopeful. I shared my intuition with David, and we were both hoping that I was right.

At about eleven thirty, I saw Heidi's number appear on my phone.

"Hey, Heidi," I answered.

"Hi, Kimberly, how are you?"

"I'm good, but I'm hoping I'll be better after this call." We both laughed.

"Well, I won't prolong this," she said. She held a torturously long pause before laughing out loud. "I would love to go through this journey with you."

I was screaming internally, my heart was racing, and after one big fist pump, I managed to say in a calm voice, "Thank you so much. I was hoping that you would say yes, but now that it's official, my heart is full." My tears were already starting to fall.

She went on to say, "My son and daughter were already aware of our meeting yesterday, so when I got home and told them what a nice couple you were, they were completely on board." We spoke briefly about the next steps but knew that Attorney Jackson had our backs.

"I'll talk to you soon," was the last thing I said before the call ended.

I had been close-lipped about the surrogacy process. I'd given very little information to my family and friends over the years. Part of it was still due to shame. I didn't know a single person who'd ever done this, so I was very selective with whom I chose to discuss it with. I was still trying to find peace in this decision. The last thing I needed was negativity from someone else. After giving David the official news of Heidi's decision, he was just as excited as I, but our hearts were both guarded.

I immediately reached out to my siblings. Through the years, they'd been a source of strength for me. I don't know what I would have done without them. I let them know that we had decided to go back down this road. I knew they would pray for us; that's what we needed most.

I also spoke with my soror, Vapes, and she was as excited as ever. From the beginning, she'd walked with me on my surrogacy journey, never questioning our decision, only being a listening ear when things got tough.

"Girl, I am so happy that you decided to try this again," she said.

"Thanks, Vapes. I don't want to get too happy, but this feels different." I knew she'd heard this before, but like a friend, she didn't mind hearing it again.

I reached out to Sherry; she had been the person who encouraged my openness to this unconventional bridge to motherhood.

"Make sure you keep me updated on every process," she said. "I believe it will work this time." She was one of my biggest cheerleaders.

Last but not least, I called my mom, but that was only to feel the love. I hadn't given her even the slightest clue that I was ever considering surrogacy or adoption. My mom loved me with a mother's love. She hurts when I hurt, so I felt the best thing for me to do was to say nothing until I had something definitive.

While we were still on the phone, Attorney Jackson called, which abruptly ended my call with my mom. She was beside herself. She'd already spoken to Heidi.

"I know this has been a long time coming, but after Heidi told me she wasn't moving forward with the other couple, then

Michael handed me the message that you'd called, I took this as a sign from God," she said.

I was blessed to have her in my corner. She was representing all sides. I knew that once she drew up the contracts, she would do what was fair for all involved.

## CHAPTER 16

# SO FAR, SO GOOD

We were so excited things seemed to be coming together for us. We prayed it would be smooth sailing from here on out. We'd all been down this road before, so we were able to set reasonable expectations and purposed to work around each other's schedule.

At the time, David focused on April 19, the date he would give my, I mean, his speech, in hopes of becoming a delegate for Georgia's Sixth District. Neither of us had ever given much attention to politics other than being avid voters and attending the last inauguration.

The morning of April 19 arrived, and David gave a rousing speech at the Precinct Caucus about what it meant to him to be able to cast a vote for the current president. Between his million-dollar speech, written by yours truly, and campaign strategy to secure votes, he became one of the delegates. He was thrilled. After his win, I submitted my paperwork in hopes of becoming a volunteer for the North Carolina convention.

Once we'd gotten through that, the next step was for us to meet with a psychologist. Of course, we chose to reach back out to Dr. Whaley.

"Kimberly, Heidi, and Davids, I wish you great success," Dr. Whaley said at the end of it all. All three meetings went off without a hitch. As we were exiting our final group session, Dr. Whaley pulled me to the side.

"Promise me you'll bring the baby over to see me?" She smiled, then gave me a warm hug.

"I promise," I assured her.

Once cleared by Dr. Whaley, I immediately put us on the calendar with Dr. Cohen. It was the day of the work-up. Heidi had been cleared less than six months ago for the other couple, so we didn't see any reason Dr. Cohen would find anything wrong. Heidi's appointment was at 10:00 a.m. in mid-May. This time David and I decided to wait for the call.

As I was about to walk into a client meeting, my phone rang. I could see it was Dr. Cohen's office.

"Hello," I said.

"Hello, Kimberly, this is Dr. Cohen. How are you?"

"I'm doing well, and hopefully I will still be doing well after this call," I laughed.

"Well, this is one time I wished you'd come in to see me," she sighed. My heart sank. "The one time that I could give you definitive good news, you don't show up." I breathed a sigh of relief.

"So, everything looks fine?" I asked.

"Things look great. We'll wait for the blood work, and if all goes well, we'll set up the protocol."

On June 4, we celebrated the birthday of yours truly. David took me to see Fatima, a jeweler friend of his, and he asked me to pick out any piece of jewelry I wanted.

"I want you to pick out something beautiful." He smiled.

"Okay, if you insist," I joked. I picked out a heart-shaped diamond pendant that included my birthstone.

"Excellent choice," said Fatima. I couldn't help but notice all the beautiful pieces of jewelry. As I moved around the case, I saw the most handsome men's watch. It was perfect. It would make for a great birthday gift for David.

"Hey, what do you think about this watch?" I playfully asked.

"I like it. I like it a lot," he responded.

Fatima smiled at me and said, "If you get it, I'll make you a good deal."

"I have a feeling I already know what I'm getting for my birthday." David grinned. He and I weren't big on surprises. We'd both rather get what the other wants.

Things were moving along quickly. Behind the scenes, Attorney Jackson was dotting every "i" and crossing every "t." On June 5, we signed the contract.

Once Heidi's next cycle began, it was time for the meds and then the transfer. David and I only had two frozen embryos left, and from everything I'd read, it was best to use both. I was no spring chicken when we created the embryos, so to me, it was unlikely that we'd have multiples.

But per the agreement, Heidi was specific about one embryo. I wanted things to move forward, so we decided to do whatever it took for her to feel comfortable. If it didn't work, we would certainly try again, and if it did, we would donate the remaining embryo to Snow Babies.

CHAPTER 17

# KEEPING BUSY

We scheduled the transfer for August 20. I had also gotten the green light to work as a volunteer for the convention in Charlotte, North Carolina. With so many things happening for us, it was hard to stay focused on the main event. By now, we'd been disappointed so many times, so it was nice that we were creating other memories to fall back on. We were in a good place.

The weekend before the transfer, David had to attend a delegate meeting in Savannah, Georgia. Of course, I went along for the ride. It was my first time in this city. Between beignets at Huey's and service at The First African Baptist Church, Savannah had it all.

During the meeting, the delegates received a sign that read, "I'm There." The goal was to take pictures with as many people as possible while holding the sign.

I thought it was a little silly, but David was on board. He must have taken pictures with half of Savannah.

As we ate dinner on the Riverwalk, at Vic's, it started to sink in that, in less than forty-eight hours, we would be embarking on another possibility of having a child together. We talked about that possibility for most of the ride back to Atlanta. We'd chosen to keep pressing toward the mark, and there was no turning back now.

The morning of the transfer, we arrived at 10:15. While we sat in the waiting room, I became overwhelmed with emotion. Why had we done this again? Hadn't we learned from the past? Just as I was about to travel full force down Pity Lane, the nurse called our names.

"Hello, Dr. and Mrs. Gowdy?"

"Yes," David answered.

"The doctor is ready for you." We nervously entered the room.

Heidi was lying with her feet in stirrups. She smiled as soon as she saw me, and I did the same.

"We just did a trial run," said Dr. Cohen. "I needed to get a sense of the layout before I included the embryo." Another familiar face came out of the adjoining room. Dr. Singh had been there from the beginning. He was the one who explained the condition of my eggs when I was concerned that so few embryos had survived. He could see the beauty of life in two hundred cells or less.

"Hello," said Dr. Singh.

"Hello," David and I chimed.

"I want you to take a look at your two embryos. Since you're only using one, I would suggest you go with the one on the right. That one appears to have slightly hatched." He spoke very matter-of-factly. They both looked the same to us, but we agreed.

David and I stood on one side of Heidi, and her David stood on the other. The lights were dim, and only Dr. Cohen's eyes peered above her mask. She looked over at David and me. I knew she could sense my anxiety. I shouldn't be anxious for nothing, but at this moment, my husband's strength had to support both of us.

"Dr. Singh," she called out.

As he walked from the other room, I had chosen the right song to play in my head—*Victory is mine.*

After the transfer, David and I went back to the waiting room. I chose to stand. David sat down and started rummaging through his briefcase.

I knew what was coming next. He'd told me a hundred times what he was going to do.

The door sprung open; it was Dave and Heidi.

"I want to take a picture of the four of us," David requested. A nurse walking in the hall agreed to take the picture. Just as he promised, David handed Heidi the small poster that read, "I'm There." She held the poster and smiled. She and Dave were good sports. Now it was time for me to rummage through my bag.

"What are you looking for, sweetie?" David asked.

"I'm looking for a piece of gum." I slyly handed the pregnancy tests to Heidi. We were already preparing for the pee test.

It was hard to think of anything other than the transfer. David and I tried to remain guarded, but we were in too deep at this point. It was only Tuesday, just one day since the transfer, so our first unofficial test wasn't until Saturday, August 25. I spoke with Heidi earlier, checking to make sure she felt okay. My close friends and family knew that I'd found a surrogate, but I was vague on the timeline of the transfer.

I was also ambiguous about Heidi's appearance. I remembered my initial reaction when I found out Heidi was white. I didn't harbor a racist bone in my body, or I would never have submitted to this process, but I wanted to see myself. I'm a black woman; I wanted an extension of me.

Luckily, another healthy distraction came along to help keep my mind busy.

"David, I just got the itinerary for my volunteer activities!" I was excited, to say the least. By the time September 4 rolled around, we'd be in North Carolina, surrounded by fellow Americans who were excited about re-electing the current president. I was a volunteer, which, of course, was not as important as being a delegate, but I'm sure volunteering also had its privileges.

A few months prior, David and I had decided to relocate permanently to Alpharetta. The traveling back and forth to Tifton had taken a toll. Regardless of the outcome with Heidi, our plan B was to buy our dream home and enjoy the fruits of our labor. But even without the traveling, life was still busy.

In preparation for the convention, I spent time frantically trying to find the right gown for the Georgia Gala. It was my dream to meet Congressman John Lewis, and he was a confirmed attendee, so I wanted to look my best.

Friday-night dining in Alpharetta was always a fun time, but where to go was always a challenge. Just too many choices.

"Hey, let's go to our usual spot," David said.

"Yum. Sounds good to me." I would have agreed to anything at this point. My focus was on the next morning and the unofficial pregnancy results.

I woke up bright and early Saturday morning. My coffee maker had already brewed my coffee; I could smell it from upstairs. No sooner than I started pouring it, I heard a beep on my phone. I looked at the clock on the oven. It was seven thirty. I walked over to the phone, and the message sent me reeling.

Just two words changed my entire morning. "Nothing yet." I knew it was a little early to test, but so many women were sending pics at 5dpt that I had just assumed the test would be positive. To say that my mood completely changed is putting it mildly. I walked into the powder room, sat on the toilet, and cried. I had to make sure David didn't hear me. I couldn't ruin his day the way mine had just crumbled.

That evening we decided to grab a bite at a spot just around the corner.

"So, what's going on with this mood of yours?" David asked.

"Nothing. Just feeling a little under the weather, I guess," I lied.

"You seem sad, not sick." He was concerned.

"I think I'm just a little anxious about next week. By next Thursday at this time, we'll either be popping a bottle of champs or drowning in our tears," I lamented.

"Can I take your order?" a young server asked, breaking the conversation.

That night we ate, talked, and laughed. David had managed to put a smile on my face. As we made our way home, I was feeling a bit better.

"Tonight was just what the doctor ordered," I said.

"Now that's what I like to hear. Glad to see you're not still 'under the weather,'" David joked.

The next morning, we'd planned to go to church. I woke up and looked over at David. The sound of his snoring was unbearable. I wanted to nudge him to make the madness go away, but the smell cascading up the steps got my attention. Aaah, the aroma of french roast was beckoning me. I reached for my phone and slipped it into my pocket to take it with me downstairs.

That first sip of coffee was just amazing. A good dose of french vanilla coffee creamer didn't hurt either. I looked at the clock. I couldn't believe it was already 8:30. I could hear the sound of rain hitting the house. I hated to admit it, but I honestly thought about getting back into bed.

A thought hit me like a bag of bricks. The test! I snatched my phone out of my pocket. I saw a message from Heidi. I paused. I was beyond scared. By day six, we should see *something*. I took a deep breath and concluded that even if it were negative, it would be okay. We were still very early. I opened the message.

"Looks positive this morning. Congratulations! Have a blessed day!" her message read. I clicked on the attached picture. It was a pee stick, and I saw a second line. It was the faintest second line imaginable, but it was there. I stared at that stick for what seemed like hours.

David didn't know what I had planned. I'd chalked up my newfound happiness to his words of encouragement. Days seven, eight, and nine, flew by, and all was fine. The line was getting darker day by day.

## CHAPTER 18

# IS SHE?

I was unofficially pregnant. Tomorrow would be the call. The pregnancy would be official.

That afternoon, I met with a client for lunch to iron out a difficult negotiation. I'd been negotiating insurance deals for twenty-five years, and I still loved it. We had just agreed on a mutual piece of business, and I was feeling great. I had been glancing at my phone all morning, almost willing it to ring. I'd kept it out of sight for the meeting, but I was sure to put it on vibrate. There was no way I was going to miss this call.

As we stood to leave, I could feel the vibration in my purse.

"So sorry, Chris, but I'm expecting a call. I need to check my phone," I said hurriedly.

"No worries," Chris said.

I could see it was Dr. Cohen's office. "Hello?" I was nervous.

"Hello, Kimberly, it's Carla. Dr. Cohen needs to speak with you."

"Oh, uh, okay." I was hoping Chris didn't see my heart beating out of my chest. "Chris, I need to take this call; I'm on hold," I said apologetically.

"I understand," Chris said. We were both making our way out the door when a familiar voice chimed in.

"Hello, Kimberly. It's Dr. Cohen."

I froze. "Dr. Cohen, I'm sorry. I'm walking out of a restaurant. Can you give me a moment?" I said.

"Okay," was her response.

"Thanks, Chris, I'll call you," I shouted as I headed to my car. "So sorry about that. I was with a client," I apologetically said.

Dr. Cohen didn't miss a beat. "We did the blood draw for Heidi this morning," she said, then paused. "Congratulations!"

Although I'd been staring at positive tests for the last five days, her words made it official. I climbed into my car, but I knew trying to drive at that moment would be futile. My tears had completely impaired my vision.

"Thank you so much, Dr. Cohen. I can't believe it," I cried.

"Believe it," she said. "The numbers look good. We'll do another test in forty-eight hours to confirm they're doubling, but I like what I see right now."

I heard someone whisper in the background, and Dr. Cohen spoke again. "Sorry, Carla just corrected me. Heidi's confirmed for Monday, September 3, since we don't draw over the weekend."

"Can I do the honors of calling Heidi?" I asked.

"Of course. It's your pregnancy news."

I thanked her a million times before we hung up. I called Heidi, and we screamed, cried, and thanked God for what we already knew.

"I can't thank you enough," I said.

"You already have," Heidi responded. Since I was already at the Perimeter, I decided to make my first purchase. I found the perfect little onesie. The pattern was a sports theme. Everybody loves sports, so it was perfect. I made a quick stop on the way home, and I had the onesie folded tight and then placed it in a small box. I knew exactly how I would surprise David.

That evening David and I decided to throw some salmon on the grill. David was grilling on our patio just off the kitchen, and I had just brought the prepared salad outside.

"I assumed we would know something about Heidi by now. Have you heard anything?" he asked.

"I thought I told you, the office changed the date to tomorrow." I snickered to myself. "On a Saturday?" he asked. "I think

Heidi had a conflict." Please, Lord, forgive me for all this dishonesty.

"I was hoping we would have found out something before we left," David said. He sounded irritated.

"David, I was looking at pictures of all the delegates and political figures. They looked so distinguished," I quizzically stated.

"Most of them are a hundred years old. They should look distinguished," David shot back, and we both laughed.

"Well, I want to give you an early birthday present. I think it would look good with your blue suit." I was excited. I placed a small felt, burgundy box on the patio table.

"Is this where I act surprised?" he asked. "I knew you were getting me that watch the moment you saw it," he said very matter-of-factly.

"Okay, you got me," I said playfully. David picked up the box and flipped it open. He squinted his eyes, trying to identify what was in front of him. The cotton material wasn't even close to the satin jewelry cloth that usually accompanied Fatima's more exclusive collections.

He picked up the material. He wasn't quite sure how to hold it. As he held the very edges of this bizarre piece of cotton, he finally turned it right side up.

"Is this a baby?" His voice trailed off, and it hit him. He looked at me as if I'd zapped him with a stun gun, eyes and mouth wide open. He asked, "Is she pregnant?"

I nodded my head as the tears streamed down my face. "Yes," I said. We stood on the patio, with tears streaming down both our faces, locked in an embrace for what seemed like hours.

# CHAPTER 19

# CIVIC DUTY

That Monday morning, David and I headed to North Carolina. The convention didn't start until Tuesday, but we both had to pick up our credentials, and I needed to get my volunteer assignments. It was a straight shot up Interstate 85. Three hours later, we were in the heart of Charlotte, North Carolina.

Since it was too early for check-in, the hotel secured an area in a back room off the lobby to secure our luggage. The hotel was just a train ride away from the credentialing sites. The committee gave us specific instructions on what to do upon arrival.

We spent the morning standing in line, getting all of our information. Delegates had prime spots and multiple checkpoints. Volunteers had maybe three checkpoints and lines that wrapped around the building; funny how that works. As I waited in line to receive my packet of information, my phone rang. I looked down at the phone.

"David, it's Dr. Cohen's office," I whispered. "Hello," I said anxiously.

"Hello, Kimberly, this is Carla."

"Hi," I said in a rushed voice. I wanted her to get on with it.

"Dr. Cohen said the numbers are perfect," she said. "They've more than doubled. Congratulations!"

"Thank you so much. So, what happens next?" I gave David the thumbs-up sign since I couldn't have the phone on speaker.

"She'll see your surrogate back here in about three weeks for the ultrasound. You all can coordinate so that you can be here," she suggested. I repeatedly thanked her. I made a mental note to call Heidi later that day.

That evening we dressed in our best attire for the Georgia Gala. I had a chance to see a lot of the state and local representatives of Georgia mixing, mingling, and drinking champagne. I also had the honor of meeting Dr. Joseph Lowery and his wife. We took pictures to commemorate the occasion.

Then I spotted him, John Lewis, chatting it up with a well-known local radio personality. David and I sashayed over in his direction. We tried to appear nonchalant, but as if by fate, my eyes met his. He nodded toward David and me.

"Hello, Mr. Lewis. It's so nice to meet you," I blurted out. I greeted the radio personality as well. David followed suit. We spent nearly fifteen minutes talking about civil rights and remembering his fateful day crossing the bridge in Selma. It's one thing to read about it, but I had the benefit of hearing it firsthand.

As I looked around the room, I admired the beauty of diversity. I was one of many African Americans conversing, laughing, and enjoying being on one accord and representing the state of Georgia, a deep Southern state that had come a long way. It made me smile.

The next few days of the convention flew by. For me, the convention was a success. I worked security, keeping order and directing the many participants. I also participated in a few events.

David and a few of his fellow delegates bragged about their access to so many famous people. He was constantly texting me pics of his encounters with the who's who.

One of the highlights was the women's conference; I worked security. Just before the conference started, David and his crew decided to leave and head over to the convention center for the "real" meetings. Just after they left, a bunch of men in dark suits started walking up and down the aisle. They asked a few security volunteers, including me, to stand in the front of the room. We stood there like a barrier.

"Wow, maybe someone important is about to speak," I said to one of the other volunteers. A door directly behind me opened. Those same men—Secret Service, I surmised at this point—walked out, and I saw them—First Lady Michelle Obama in a colorful, sleeveless dress, and Dr. Jill Biden in a black fitted dress, also sleeveless. They were about ten feet away from me. My heart was pounding. Both women spoke, and the crowd responded positively to every word.

I wanted an opportunity to meet them. Dr. Biden had already been whisked away, likely for another event, but the First Lady stepped down from the stage. As the Secret Service watched every movement of anyone who came close to her, it was she who gently nodded her head in their direction to allow her fellow Americans a chance to shake hands, embrace, and, likely, express their love and admiration for what they believed she and her husband meant to this country. I waited with anticipation for her to make her way down the line. Finally, she was standing right in front of me.

As she extended her hand, she uttered, "Thank you so much for your support; it means a lot."

I nodded at her words and barely managed to say, "You're welcome." The moment was surreal. I was disappointed that the guy behind me failed to capture the handshake, but I'd captured so many pictures of her that my proximity to her was clear. I knew David would be livid that he didn't get a chance to meet her, which is why I immediately sent him a text and a picture with the caption, "Michelle sends her love."

## CHAPTER 20

# I'VE GOT NEWS FOR YOU

Now that the high from the convention was over, all of our attention was focused on Baby Gowdy. I was attending the first ultrasound the next morning. I had been on pins and needles after the transfer, but the anticipation had jumped up a level. Tomorrow I would hopefully see a flicker of a heartbeat. Glimpses of past failures tried to creep into my mind, but I kept praying that we'd have good news. That was all I could do.

The Davids had decided to sit this one out. This day would be a moment for Heidi and me.

"Kimberly, you can come back," a short, heavy-set nurse directed. Heidi was draped in a sheet and lying on the table in a dimly lit room. The moment the condom-covered wand was in place, all eyes became fixated on the monitor. I heard the word yolk sac and a few other things, but my eyes transfixed on the flickering light. I'd seen that light before. Baby Gowdy had made it to another milestone—the heartbeat. Only this time, I prayed we'd placed the baby in a better vessel.

"I printed out two sets of pictures. Is that okay?" the technician asked.

"Absolutely," I said. After the appointment, Heidi and I sat in the lobby looking at the pictures. At six weeks along, I was already in love with my baby.

"Oh look, he has my eyes," I said, and we both laughed. The appointment was a success. I couldn't wait to get home to show David.

David was ecstatic. "This is our time, Kimberly. I know you were apprehensive about moving forward, but thank you for trusting me on this," he said.

We both knew the next step. It was time to share our good news. I'd made this type of announcement too many times. The first time Reggie and I saw a positive pregnancy test was the most exciting time ever. Two years into our marriage, it was time for the pitter-patter of little feet. My in-laws wanted a grandchild right after they heard the words "I do." But Reggie and I had decided to enjoy married life for at least a year. After the second year with no birth control, we both thought something might be wrong, but shortly after, we finally saw the plus sign. We were ready to tell the world.

We shared the news with close family and friends, but word got around. Had I known about my propensity for a miscarriage, I would have kept quiet.

Our parents were overjoyed back then, especially my mother-in-law. I hadn't even made it to the first ultrasound and she was already talking about baby names. About two weeks later, I started spotting. The doctor ordered me to come in for an ultrasound to make sure all was okay. I'd already started reading books, so I knew a little about what to expect. The sac and the heartbeat meant I was okay.

As I lay there, I watched the technician's face. She kept moving the vaginal wand and asking questions.

"When was your last cycle?" she asked. "Do you think we could be a little early? Are you sure the test was positive?" Our happiness was short-lived when they determined that I'd had a chemical pregnancy. I had never heard this term before.

Delivering the news was painful. My mom and dad shared my pain, but my mother-in-law was heartbroken. She was also suspicious. She contended that she'd had a miscarriage in her own life, that it was an awful experience, and that I should be cramping, bleeding, and passing the tissue. My doctor had to explain to her that back when she was bearing children, there were no tests confirming pregnancy the first day of a missed period. A late period that may have been heavier than normal was sometimes a miscarriage, but because the woman had no idea she was pregnant in the first place, she chalked it up to a late period. She ultimately understood, but the feeling that I had failed her and so many others lingered.

The evening after Heidi's ultrasound, with a glass of my favorite red blend, I started making calls.

"Mom, guess what? I know this is going to sound a little strange to you, and I'm not sure how you will respond, but David and I decided to use a surrogate to have a baby," I finally said.

"A surrogate? I think I saw something like that on TV. A mom was the surrogate for her daughter." She sounded somewhat confused.

"Yes, we found someone who will carry our child."

"So, what if she doesn't want to give her child away? I don't know about this. You've been through so much with the other babies. I don't want you to be hurt," she cried.

"Mom, it's different now." I proceeded to enlighten her on all the ways that technology had advanced.

"My God, what are they gonna think of next?" She continued, "So now that you've found somebody, you're going to plant the baby to see if it grows?" *Implant is the term, but I guess you could call it planting*, I thought.

"We've already completed that process." I paused. "Our surrogate is already pregnant, and the baby is already growing," I added that last line for effect. I could hear my mom take a long inhale before she let out an even longer exhale.

"I know how much you want a child. I've been there with you from the beginning. There is nothing more that I want for you than to see you happy and to raise a child of your own. I don't know a lot about this surrogacy stuff, but if this means that you have a chance to get your blessing, then I'll pray and ask the Lord to bless you and David, and bless the woman carrying my grandbaby."

Thirty minutes and box of tissues later, my mom and I hung up. My dad was a laid-back kind of guy, always cool, calm, and collected.

"What?! Baby girl, that's great news!" he exclaimed. "What! Surrogate? Are you kidding? I can't believe it! What! My, my, my. Where's David? Baby girl, I'm just so happy for you." The conversation went on like this for about ten minutes until I finally got the nerve to say goodbye to my calm, cool, and collected dad.

My sisters and girlfriends were ecstatic as well. I was asked to give them the rundown.

"So, how did you meet her?" "What's her name?" "What is she like?" "Is she married?" "How old is she?" I gladly answered all their questions, but in each setting, I saved her name and her race for last. It didn't matter to me, and I was hoping it didn't matter to anyone else. Just as I suspected, to all those who had walked with me all these years, Heidi's race was a non-issue. They were happy at the chance that I could become a mom. I relished knowing that so many people were cheering for us.

David spoke with Diana and his girls, Angela and Gabrielle. It didn't go as well as he expected. Although David and I had been married for years at that point, my relationship with them was not quite warm and fuzzy. They'd always been daddy's girls, and that wouldn't change, but even grown children like to see their parents together.

"They'll come around," David said. He was sure of it. David's cousin, Dr. Pearl, was ecstatic. She loved her cousin like a brother. If anyone had his back, it was her. She knew how much the possibility of a son meant to him, and he had a fifty-fifty chance.

We took a drive down to Florida. David wanted to speak with his dad and stepmom, Bernice, in person. His parents had divorced years before we met, but his love for his dad and stepmom was strong. I shared that sentiment and lovingly referred to them as Mom and Dad.

His dad, Josh, had just turned eighty-seven the month before, so we thought we'd have to explain exactly *how* we were pregnant. We couldn't have been more wrong.

"That is a beautiful thing," his dad said.

"I am so happy for you, and I can't wait to meet this baby," Mom sighed. We talked about Heidi and Dave and sang their praises, then we decided to show them the picture of the four of us holding the "I'm There" sign. I knew that David's parents grew up in a different time, a time when the world was even less friendly to people of color. Dad had even fought in a segregated army in World War II. However, once they saw Heidi's picture, none of that mattered.

"Well now, what a nice lady to do something so special," Dad said.

"I see the world is changing." Mom smiled. We enjoyed our time in Florida. We feasted on Dad's great breakfast of ackee and saltfish with cornbread on the side. We'd always enjoyed our time in Florida, and this time was no different.

## CHAPTER 21

# THE TRANSITION

Now that Heidi was eight weeks, it was time to transition to her OB-GYN. Heidi had assured me that her OB was surrogacy friendly. She spoke highly of the team of doctors and told me they'd helped make her previous surrogacy a success. During that pregnancy, she delivered via C-section. It was the expertise of this practice that had allowed an optimal outcome. I was excited about attending that first visit and as many subsequent visits as possible.

David and I were sitting in the parking lot when we saw Heidi exit the car. We'd decided to meet her for an early-morning doctor visit. Heidi's Dave had to work, but we promised him we'd take good care of her. All the paperwork and ultrasound pictures had been sent over from Dr. Cohen's office. This first visit was for David and me to meet the new medical team, set up the insurance payment schedule, and take a peek at Baby Gowdy.

As we entered the office, we noticed that a large, rectangular-shaped receptionist station sat in the center of the room. The station was overwhelming. David and I took a seat as Heidi confirmed her arrival. Since this was Heidi's current OB doctor, they already had her medical history, so there wasn't much paperwork to consider.

As we sat there waiting to hear Heidi's name called, I glanced over at a young couple sitting in the corner of the room. She was pregnant, rubbing her large belly and wearing what looked like house slippers. She noticed that I did a double-take at her feet.

"I know having on house shoes looks bad," she said. "But it's the only thing that will fit my feet at this point." We all laughed.

"Please forgive me for staring," I exhaled.

"Are you pregnant?" she asked. This was the moment of truth. What do I say right here and right now? Before I could say anything, David responded.

"Yes, but we're only two months along." Heidi and I slyly looked at each other.

"Good answer," I said, but David looked at me and smiled.

"Not a *good* answer; it's *the* answer." I was still giving kudos to David when a young nurse called out.

"Heidi?"

As Heidi rose, she signaled for us to follow suit. I noticed that the nurse, as well as the reception staff, were all looking at us. They were staring at us as inappropriately as I'd done to the woman with the slippers. Maybe it was just my imagination.

Just before the nurse, Polly, allowed us back, she gave us a once-over and a confused stare. I guess I needed to get used to it. She took us back to a small conference room. Shortly after that, Dr. Hall walked in. He was a white man, average height, with salt-and-pepper '80s hair, much like John Travolta in *Staying Alive*. He looked to be in his early sixties.

"Hello, Heidi." He hugged her. "I see here we have the Gowdys, correct?"

"Yes," David and I both responded.

"Heidi informed us about the surrogacy arrangement." He smiled.

"Other than Heidi, have you had other surrogacy cases?" David asked.

"One other besides Heidi, and things went well. Heidi may have told you that we are surrogacy friendly," he was proud to say.

"What exactly does that mean?" I asked.

"We make sure the IPs feel a part of the process, just as if they would if you were carrying the child. We understand that by the time you've taken this route, you've gone through quite a few bumps and bruises. We try to keep that thought in the forefront."

We talked about the rotation of the doctors, the scheduled doctor visits, and what to expect at each visit. He also advised us that the front desk would be handling the financial arrangements. We were fortunate that Heidi had her own insurance. That was a selling point with Attorney Jackson. However, David and I were responsible for any out-of-pocket costs incurred by Heidi like copays, deductibles, and coinsurances incurred as a result of the baby.

Now it was time to take a look at Baby Gowdy. The ultrasound would be David's first time seeing the heartbeat. David and I held hands as Baby Gowdy was on full display. We could see the flickering. I was already in love.

"We should be able to hear something," Dr. Hall suggested. He must have turned up the volume because, suddenly, a familiar sound filled the room, a sound that I'd heard many times before. A beautiful sound.

"One hundred thirty bpm," I heard Dr. Hall say. His voice snapped me out of my trance.

"Is that good?" I asked.

"Excellent heart rate," he replied. It was time to discuss the financials with the front desk. Two of the three African American women sitting in the reception area wore bright smiles.

"I want to tell you that Heidi is the best. We were with her through her previous surrogacy," one of them said warmly. I concurred. The older black woman with her hair pulled back into a severe bun walked over and stood in front of David and me.

"I think this says a lot about you and Heidi. People are people. It doesn't matter about black or white. It's what's in the heart that matters, and don't let anybody tell you otherwise," she lectured.

David and I nodded our heads. We couldn't agree more, but

we didn't quite understand why she was so emphatic. The last of the three women had been printing out documents. She was attaching the paperwork to a clipboard. As she walked over to us, she was sure not to make eye contact. She wasn't nearly as warm as the other two.

"Please read this over and sign at the bottom," she sternly said. David and I both sensed a problem, but it wasn't ours, so we just let it go.

Other than this one hiccup, the office visit went well. Before we left, David and I took a sideview photo of Heidi. We wanted to witness the month-by-month growth of our baby.

## CHAPTER 22

# FEELING GUILTY

Over the next few months, Heidi blossomed. I was able to make it to each doctor's appointment. The office staff and doctors had grown accustomed to seeing us together. The Davids couldn't make the appointments, but I was there. If I was going to live vicariously, I had to be there.

The doctors were on rotation, so today we were meeting Dr. Kidman. Heidi and I were directed to make our way back to the examination room. Dr. Kidman entered the room. She looked to be in her late fifties, with dark-brown hair and a very petite frame. She was all smiles and very personable. Initially.

She went down the list of questions for Heidi. "How are you feeling today?" she asked.

"I'm feeling just okay," she said.

"You're getting close to the fifth-month mark, so you should start to feel pretty good," said Dr. Kidman. *That's never been my experience.*

"Any changes since your last visit? Have you felt the baby kick?" Dr. Kidman continued.

"I've felt movement, lots of movement, but no kicks," Heidi grimaced.

"Well, it's still somewhat early. Okay, let's take a listen." She directed Heidi to lie back. I took her hand as she began getting into position. Dr. Kidman squirted gel onto her growing belly. I remember how cold that gel could be.

As she rolled the doppler over Heidi's tummy, the sound of

galloping horses made its way into the room. It sent chills through my body.

"Sounds good," said the doctor.

"Do you mind if we take another listen?" I asked. Dr. Kidman glanced over at me as if I were an intruder. She looked to Heidi and asked, "Is it okay if we take another listen?"

I was livid! Hearing the heartbeat was my moment. This was my child. Heidi could see the look on my face. She and I had already talked about how important this appointment was for me, and so before I turned into KimISHA, Heidi spoke up.

"Of course it's okay if Kimberly wants to hear her child's heartbeat," Heidi said softly. Dr. Kidman looked at me. She could see the pain she had just caused. My eyes had started to fill with tears.

"Kimberly, I'm so sorry. I was on call all night, and now I'm filling in for another doctor this morning. I'm just not myself," she exhaled. That changed the mood entirely. Soon the sound of galloping horses could be heard again, and all was right with the world.

"Have you all thought about a quad marker screening?" asked Dr. Kidman.

"No," I said. "I remember Dr. Hall suggesting an amniocentesis because of my age, but we'd decided not to do it." I was starting to feel included.

"I would recommend the marker screening," Dr. Kidman said. "It's noninvasive, it can check for neural-tube defects like brain and spine development, and it can also check for Down syndrome."

"As long as its noninvasive, I'm okay with it. I don't want Heidi to go through too much," I said.

"Excellent, I'll give you the order for the ultrasound, but I'd like to have the blood draw completed today. We like to do this between fifteen and twenty weeks, so that only gives us two weeks before we're outside of the window." I nodded my head in agreement. She extended her hand to Heidi to help her sit up, gave me a smile and a wink, and then left the room.

"Thank you so much for having my back, Heidi," I said.

"Kimberly, this is your baby, even though I'm carrying him ... or her," she quickly corrected. "You are still in charge." At that moment, I admired Heidi even more.

That night I shared what happened with David. He was as supportive as ever. He went on to co-sign the long hospital hours and how exhaustion was one of the problems within the medical field. I gave him the date, time, and place for the marker test.

"Hey, what's going on with you?" David asked. He knew me so well.

"Today, standing in the examination room with Heidi, I started feeling guilty. I was happy, but thoughts of Elijah flooded my mind. He was the closest that I'd ever come to becoming a mom. I stood there feeling like I was dishonoring him, as if the new baby was taking his place. Why hadn't I given him a healthy environment to thrive?" I cried.

"Listen," David said. "We can all love more than one person at a time. The love I feel for this baby takes nothing away from Angela and Gabrielle." He continued, "Think about it like this. If I passed away and you miraculously found someone as intelligent, as loving, and as perfect as me—" He snickered.

"Let me get my boots out," I laughed.

"Seriously, your love for this baby takes nothing away from Elijah, and as far as giving him a better environment, only God can see the end from the beginning. You had no way of knowing the outcome."

David could always make me feel better, even if I did have to wear boots from time to time.

CHAPTER 23

# TELL US HOW YOU *REALLY* FEEL

David and I had planned to hang out with friends the weekend before the ultrasound. Preparing for Baby Gowdy had consumed us so much that we hadn't given much time to enjoy our friendships.

Rashad and Janet were friends of David's. Rashad was a doctor, and his wife, Janet, was a real estate agent. Once I met Janet, we all became fast friends. We were currently working with Janet to find our dream home.

I'd known Troy and Halle from Connecticut. They both worked in the insurance industry. Once Troy accepted the position as the Southeast regional director, they decided to move to Atlanta. Halle was a stay-at-home mom, with the hardest job of any of us. I could always count on them for a good Sunday dinner, but I limited my interaction with them mainly to home-cooked meals. As a single woman, I didn't feel comfortable always being the third wheel.

Then there was Marvin and Geena. They were both a ball of fun. Marvin was a college professor, and Geena was a nurse who worked with David. David had known Marvin since childhood when he moved to Atlanta. It was David who put in a good word for Geena at the hospital.

We all lived in the Alpharetta–Johns Creek area, but we decided to meet up in Buckhead. We had more options, as any

Buckhead-area restaurant would do the trick. David and I barely arrived on time. Marvin and Geena were already sitting in the lobby.

"Hey, man, how you doin'?" Marvin and David both shook hands, leaned in, and slapped each other on the back in a bromance kind of way. Geena and I greeted each other with a warm hug.

"So, I hear you and David have been busy," she said as Troy and Halle walked in.

"Hey everybody, sorry we're late," said Halle. She was a sweetheart. The hugs continued with the six of us. Rashad and Janet were habitually late, so we asked the hostess if we could be seated without the entire party present. The hostess agreed.

Once seated, it was time to catch up. Each of us gave a high-level overview of what was happening in our lives.

"May I take your drink orders?" a young, attractive Middle Eastern server asked. We each placed our orders and continued with the conversation.

David looked up from his menu. "There they are," he shouted. Rashad and Janet were walking toward the table. Janet was always impeccably dressed, nails, hair, and shoes always on point. Once we climbed out from under all these fertility bills, I was going to step it up.

The server quickly returned with our drinks and took drink orders from Rashad and Janet. After we'd all placed our food orders, laughed, and had enjoyed our second glass of wine, the conversation turned to David and me.

"How do you feel about the whole surrogacy process?" Geena asked.

"I feel fine. Things are going well," I responded.

"Heidi has been a blessing to us, and we couldn't have asked for anyone better," David chimed.

"Heidi? That's a weird name for a sistah," Janet joked. The entire table laughed.

"Heidi's not black," I said. "She and her husband, David, are white." The table was momentarily silent.

"Oh, okay. I just assumed, but I see no problem with that," said Janet.

"I'm surprised," added Halle. "Is that why none of us have met her?"

"Surprised at what?" I shot back.

"It's just that I would never have thought that you and David would be open to crossing over."

"Crossing over to what?" I said. "The child is biologically ours; she's just carrying him." I started to get irritated.

"I know this might sound weird, but won't the baby have her blood?" asked Troy.

Rashad burst out laughing. "You can't be serious?" he asked Troy.

"No, I'm very serious!" Troy shot back.

"Wait, wait, wait." David decided to take control of the table. "Yes, Heidi is white, but the egg and the sperm determine the DNA. This will be a little black kid, the same as Kimberly and me." He hoped this would be the end of it. He was wrong.

"I just get tired of the white savior narrative," Halle blurted out.

"What is that supposed to mean?" I asked.

"Every time you see a movie, it's some white person going into the inner city and saving all the black people. Now they're trying to save the educated ones too." She seemed very upset.

"First of all, do you know how many black women we chose to go down this road with before Heidi?" I said. I was livid and KimISHA was now on full display. "There were three other women, all black, who we hoped could help us. Not to mention the countless discussions with other black women before I realized things wouldn't work out." My voice was getting louder.

"Did I want to go down this road of surrogacy?" I continued, barely taking a breath. "No, but it's easy for you to judge as you sit in the country club with three beautiful kids of your own. You haven't even bothered to contact us, which is why you don't know about the other women, but now you're sitting here judging us instead of being happy for us." I was hot.

"Kimberly, I don't think Halle is judging. She's just pointing out that society has always tried to place white people as heroes bailing out minorities," said Troy.

"Okay, I think you're reading way too much into this. I don't remember asking you for a penny when we decided to go down this road," offered David. Marvin and Geena had been silent until now.

"I've known David my entire life," Marvin began. "I know how he raised his children, and I know how he thinks. We need to get away from all this racial stuff. Why don't we look at the fact that Heidi clearly didn't have a problem with race? I want to think that when she saw David and Kimberly, she saw two people who needed help," he stated, but Halle wasn't having any of it.

"Just like we're asking you about her race, how do you know her family isn't disgusted that she's carrying a black baby?" she asked.

"Disgusted?!" Geena was ticked.

"I'm just sayin', they could be full of racial bias for all you know," Halle quipped.

Geena snapped. "Girl, bye! Why are you even here? You've been crazy since I met you." I knew it was my time to jump in.

"Halle, this is our decision. Let's agree to disagree." I was trying to hold back tears. Troy and Halle chose not to participate in any conversation going forward. They ate the rest of their dinner in silence. Once they paid their check, they immediately excused themselves from the table and left. I think we were all shocked it had come to this.

"Thank you all for supporting us," David said. I was just ready to go.

## CHAPTER 24

# IT'S A BOY... IT'S A GIRL

Today was the day of the infamous twenty-week ultrasound. We would finally get a chance to take a good look at Baby Gowdy. About a week before, I'd received a call from Dr. Kidman. The marker test had indicated what she considered a very minor, if any, abnormality. She kept assuring us that this test is known for its inaccuracies, but of course, that only made me wonder why we needed it in the first place.

Surprisingly, David and I didn't give the news a lot of thought. As we made our way across town, we were all smiles.

"Are you sure you put the right address in the GPS?" David snapped.

"Yes, I have the address right here," I said. It was the biggest day of this journey so far, and we were late. Ten minutes later, we found ourselves willing the elevator to hurry down and carry us up to the seventh floor.

When we stepped off the elevator, we were greeted by a young, overly polite receptionist.

"Are you the Gowdys?" she asked.

"Yes." We sounded like a chorus. She directed us down the hall. We were walking so fast we were almost running.

"Room B on your right!" the receptionist yelled. David tapped lightly on the door.

"Good morning," Heidi's David greeted us as he opened the door. When we walked into the room, a tall blonde woman in a white jacket was talking to Heidi.

I assumed it was the technician. I was right. She came over and introduced herself.

"Hello, I'm Tanora." She was very bubbly.

"We're the Gowdys," David announced.

"Well, I think we can get started. Is everybody here?" Tanora asked.

"Yes," I said. Her next comment melted my heart.

"I was ready to get started, but Heidi insisted that we wait for you," said Tanora.

I looked over at Heidi and mouthed, "Thank you."

I had grown to love Heidi. She looked out for me at every turn. We both wanted the same thing, to bring a healthy baby into the world.

"I'm going to do some measurements and give you information along the way," Tanora explained. I noticed that Heidi had gotten much bigger in just two weeks. As soon as the tech placed the paddle on Heidi's growing belly, the image of a very active Baby Gowdy was on full display. The technician took pictures, measured, and explained what we were seeing. She left the room with the pictures. Shortly after that, an older black woman with salt-and-pepper cornrows accompanied Tanora into the room.

"Hello, I'm Dr. Eli, the radiologist. Dr. Kidman told us that you were aware of a possible abnormality due to the level of one of the markers." The mood of the room changed. "There's nothing to worry about," she said. "I didn't see anything based on the pictures, but I'd like to take a look for myself to confirm. Is that okay?" she asked. We nodded.

After about ten minutes and more pictures, Dr. Eli finished her inspection.

"Everything looks good," she said. She went on to explain a little more about the multiple marker test, as it's also called. She wanted to assure us that the number was off just slightly, but with the level, coupled with the ultrasound, there was no need for concern. After Dr. Eli left the room, it was time for the moment that we'd been waiting for.

"Does anyone want to know the sex of the baby?" Tanora asked. I'd gone online almost every day, looking for ways to identify the sex of a baby. Once you see the legs in that "V" shape, you can pretty much figure it out.

"Yes, we want to know the sex of the baby." David couldn't contain himself. I could see her moving across Heidi's belly, trying to get a good view of the goods. Suddenly, I could see that my online research had paid off.

"OMG," I said. "It's a boy! I can see his pee-pee!" I'd blurted out. David looked at the tech to see if she could co-sign my internet-degree findings.

Tanora smiled and said, "Yes, she's right. It's a boy." David paced around the room, going back and forth in disbelief. He was an only child with two daughters. At least he was sure the Gowdy name could now go on. This meeting was certainly a roller-coaster ride—the high, the low, and then ending on a very big high. We thanked God for all he'd done for us, was doing, and would do going forward. After the appointment, I almost suggested we go for a chimichanga, but work was calling my name.

The following week was Christmas. We never considered putting up a tree, and this year was no different. David and I usually traveled during the holidays, but this year we stayed close to home. Even though the due date wasn't until May 7, we wanted to use this time to prepare our home for the baby. Besides, we'd already made plans to be in Washington, DC, the following month for the inauguration, and we had planned a trip to Trinidad and Tobago for Carnival. We figured we'd better get all of our travels in now because, once Baby Gowdy came, who knew the next time we'd be able to get up and go.

Over the holidays, I'd had many discussions with family and friends. They seemed to be just as excited as David and me. My mom called daily, which was her MO even before talk of the baby. My entire family circle and friends kept me going, from girls' nights to uplifting text messages or a phone call. They had my back, and I knew it.

Even my colleagues had gotten in on the fun. A few of them made bets on when Baby Gowdy would arrive. They kept a calendar in the office with everyone's prediction. The doctor had already told us that the baby would be born via C-section, but that didn't keep my team from casting their best guestimate.

David and I, on the other hand, were trying to come up with nicknames. We played around with a bunch of names. DJ was too obvious. Lil D made him sound like a would-be rapper—not that anything was wrong with being a rapper, but exactly how much street cred could a kid growing up in Johns Creek, Georgia, have? *My name is Doc. I can't find my sock. My mom used to call me the king of the block.* See what I mean?

So, we chose Doc, as a tribute to his dad. Whether he became a physician, a teacher, or an athlete, Doc would represent knowledge in whatever he became.

It was time for me to discuss "maternity leave." I wasn't quite sure how this would work, but my director left this up to me. Each year I received five weeks of vacation and could carry over one week from the previous year. Through the years, David and I had traveled, but I never seemed to put a dent in those five weeks. I think it was the nature of my job. I could work from anywhere, so even a trip to Connecticut to visit family didn't require many vacation days because it didn't keep me from working. Have Wi-Fi, will work.

After I arrived in the office, I heard a familiar voice.

"Hello, Kimberly. How are you?" I knew that voice very well, that beautiful Sierra Leone accent. I turned around to see my esteemed colleague, my fiercest competitor, Chidima.

"I'm good. How are you?"

"Great. I wanted to run something by you," she said.

"Okay, what's going on?" I asked.

"After the baby is born, I would like to have a baby naming ceremony for him. I want to give him his African name," she said.

"Wow, I would love that," I said.

"I have already picked his name, but I will not share it until the ceremony," she said.

"How does the ceremony work?" I was curious.

"It will not be a full-blown ceremony, but I will bring all the items needed. It will be the perfect name," she sighed.

I felt so honored. I gave her a warm hug. The holidays have a way of bringing out the best in people, and so does an impending birth. I was finally the recipient of all the attention, and it felt good.

# CHAPTER 25

# HERE COMES THE JUDGE

Between the excitement of the inauguration and our nonstop fun at Carnival, time had flown by. Heidi was now in her seventh month, and from the pictures she'd sent us while we were on vacation, she and Doc seemed to be coming along nicely. It was time for the Pre-Birth Order. Attorney Jackson had already prepared us for this next phase.

"This will make your baby's birthday much smoother," she advised. This order would ensure our names were listed on our son's birth certificate as his mother and father from day one. It also allowed us to make any decisions about our baby at the time of his birth. Without the Pre-Birth Order, the hospital would have to recognize Heidi and her husband as Doc's parents, at least on the birth certificate.

The good news is the contract we signed between all parties would supersede the birth certificate, of course, but that would mean going to court and requesting a Post-Birth Order to remove their names. Thank God Attorney Jackson was one of the best in the business, so she had us covered.

David and I made our way down to the Fulton County Courthouse in the heart of the ATL. We pulled into a parking deck and made our way up the ramp. Each level was as packed as the first.

"Can these people learn how to park?" David complained. Most of the cars were either too close or over the line.

"Maybe this is just payback for your driving skills," I laughed. After his quick eye roll, David pulled into a spot.

"Make sure you remember what level we're on," he said. My phone rang.

"Hello?"

"Hello, Kimberly. How are you?" It was Attorney Jackson.

"I'm doing well. We're getting ready to head over to the judge's chambers," I said.

"Excellent. I just spoke with Heidi, and she said you all are meeting in the lobby before you head up."

"Yes, we just arrived. I think we're all pretty nervous and want everything to go well." David and I had now made our way down to street level.

"You've made it through the hard part," Attorney Jackson said. "It's all gravy from here." I could tell she was excited. "I won't be able to make it to court today, but my partner, Attorney Sheila Morgan, will be there. She'll witness the judge sign the Pre-Birth Order. She'll meet you all on the seventh floor. The meeting starts in about fifteen minutes, so try to be on time. This judge is a stickler for punctuality," she said.

"We're entering the building now; I can see Heidi and Dave across the room," I informed. After a few more instructions, we said our goodbyes, and she gave her well-wishes.

"Empty all pockets, and have your bags open." Security was tight at the state building. After a quick once-over with the security wand, we were on our way. We greeted Heidi and David with the biggest hugs possible, and I thanked her again for the beautiful pics.

"Let's stand over here out of the way," I said. We all joined hands right in the lobby of the state building and prayed that all would go well.

"Amen," we said in unison. On our way up in the elevator, my stomach felt like I was on a thrill ride. We wanted this child so much; it was time to make sure the law recognized him as rightfully ours. Once the door opened, we could see Attorney Morgan leaning up against a wall, typing on her handheld. We'd only met her a few times on this journey. She reminded David and me of Meryl Streep in *Kramer vs. Kramer*. How ironic, considering today was about parental rights. I wiped that thought out of my mind.

She turned and noticed us. "I see the gang's all here," she smiled. We each greeted her.

"Thank you so much," I said nervously.

"Kimberly, I see that look on your face. There's nothing to be worried about. This is merely a formality," said Attorney Morgan. "Well, if you're ready, we can go ahead into the judge's chambers," she instructed. She took the lead, and we followed.

When I stepped into the office, I faced the side view of a huge oak desk that took up most of the space. Four Queen Anne chairs were placed directly in front of it. Degrees adorned the walls, and off to the side sat a small table with two Queen Anne chairs that completed the matching set.

"Okay, guys have a seat," Attorney Morgan instructed. Heidi and Dave sat farthest away from the door. Heidi was a pro. She'd gone through this before. I tried to pick up on her relaxed vibe, but unfortunately, it wasn't working.

"Hello, do we have everyone here?" said a tall, distinguished-looking black man as he walked through the door. We all started to stand, but he directed us to stay seated. As soon as I saw him, James Earl Jones came to mind. Not only was his voice distinct, but he had a regal presence. Thank God I'd never committed a crime. I'd hate to stand before him.

Attorney Morgan stood to the right of us next to the judge's desk, closer to Heidi and Dave. Judge Edwards took his seat.

"So, who do we have here?" he asked.

"Your Honor, we have Dr. David and Kimberly Gowdy. They're the IPs," said Attorney Morgan. David stood and shook the judge's hand, and I nodded with a smile. "We also have David and Heidi Swangel. As you can see, she's the surrogate." Dave stood and shook the judge's hand, and Heidi nodded, same as me.

"We're here today to swear before his honor the parental

intent for Baby Gowdy," said Attorney Morgan. She gestured to the judge that she had given him the floor.

"If there are no questions, I'd like to get started." He smiled. "David Gowdy, do you attest that this is your child and that you will assume full financial and legal responsibility upon his or her birth?" asked Judge Edwards.

"I do," David replied. I was asked the same question, of course, and I replied, "I do."

"Heidi, do you attest that the child you are currently carrying is not your child, that you are not the child's mother, and that you have no financial or legal obligation to him or her?" he asked.

"I do," she replied. Her David also answered, "I do," when asked the same question. My nerves had settled. This was nothing like I had imagined. The judge gave a few additional remarks and then signed the order. We all smiled and thanked him for his time. He and my David struck up a conversation, and while talking, the judge mentioned that his alma mater was Harvard, and David cited Yale as his. I had attended the oldest HBCU in the United States, Cheyney University, and was proud of it.

As they talked, my mind couldn't help but think about the dynamics of the room. Here we sat in a chamber listening to the banter of two Ivy League black men, one a judge and the other a doctor. I thought about myself as a black woman, doing extremely well in my career. The history of our country has often depicted a black woman caring for, nurturing, and acting as a wet nurse for the slave master's children, even before her own. Even a hundred years post-slavery, in the 1960s, black women with little financial means continued to be paid for their ability to provide love and care to children who were not their own.

Now here we were decades later, and strangely, this seemed to be a role reversal. I was the black woman who now had the financial means to pay a white woman to provide love and care to a child that was not her own. She'd even offered to provide my son with colostrum, the first breast milk, symbolic of a

*The Colorless Womb*

twenty-first-century wet nurse. I placed my hand on Heidi's. What a treasure I had found.

I noticed Judge Edwards take in our moment. That must have been when he decided to offer his commentary, which felt like he read my mind.

"Although our country has elected its first African American president, we still have a long way to go," he opened. "Sitting here watching the four of you and knowing the history of this country makes me proud. At the end of a long hard day, we are more alike than we are different. What matters most is what's in a man's heart."

I could see the look on Attorney Morgan's face. She wore a heartfelt smile, as did the rest of us. I was glad that we had looked past race, overlooked skin color, and recognized the colorless womb.

I left the office feeling 100 percent confident about my decision to take this journey with Heidi. After the incident with Halle and Troy, I'd questioned my choice. Halle had called me a few times, but I didn't want any negativity coming my way, so I never answered. I'd had a few other run-ins about the "consequences" of using someone outside of my race to carry my child, supposedly the stigma and the shame that my child would feel later on in life. I called "bull" on all of it. I would raise my son, just as I was raised, to love all people regardless of the color of their skin.

"You remember we still need to meet Eileen, right?" David asked, breaking my train of thought. I had forgotten about it.

"Yes, what time again?" I asked

"Two o'clock," he answered. Eileen was a maternity nurse. David knew her from the hospital. Once word got out about our surrogacy, she wanted to teach us a few techniques on how to manage a fussy baby and how to childproof our home. When I told my mom about her impending visit, she laughed.

"Are you kidding me? You're having someone teach you how to quiet a baby?" she scoffed.

"Mom, they have a lot of new techniques now," I replied.

"Chile, I had six kids, and not one time did somebody have to teach me about quieting a baby."

"But Mom," I said before she interrupted.

"I hope you're not paying for this. If so, I can come down and show you for free," she balked.

"No, but there are people who pay for these services. Teaching is her gift to us," I said.

"Boy, I tell you, the things people spend money on. What that baby will need is love, and if he's fussy, put a little cereal in the bottle and call it a day." She paused. "Childproofing a house? Huh, if you tap their hands the first time, I guarantee he won't do it again," she said.

I just let her have her say, but deep down I knew she was right. I also knew I didn't have quite the village in Atlanta I needed, so I had to get all the tips I could find.

## CHAPTER 26

# LET'S SET A DATE

Dr. Achebe was the doctor on rotation. He was a tall, slender man with a Nigerian accent.

"Everything looks fine. The size of the fundus is right on target for the due date," he said. "Where do you plan to deliver?" he asked.

"At Memorial," I answered.

"Have you already done the hospital tour?"

I looked at Heidi. "My tour is next week. I had my last surrobaby at Memorial, and it was a great experience," she said.

"I see you had a C-section with your last pregnancy," Dr. Achebe inquired.

"Yes, I did, but with my own children I had them naturally," Heidi added.

"I would say we should schedule the procedure to deliver the baby the week of the twenty-eighth of April. We like to see the baby in utero until at least thirty-nine weeks. I'll make a note of it, and you can talk to the doctor about the specifics at your next appointment."

As we made our way to the front desk, Heidi seemed distant. Usually, we would be chatting it up, but not today. I was hoping I hadn't said the wrong thing in the examination room. I'd be sure to find out what was wrong. Today was the day for me to pay the insurance deductible for the hospital, so Heidi decided to head out before me.

"I'll see you later," she said.

"Are you okay?" I asked, concerned.

"I'm fine. Just a lot on my mind."

I didn't press the issue. I hugged her, and we said our goodbyes. I chalked it up to hormones. As I waited, I noticed that the least-friendly office staffer was preparing the invoice. She walked over and handed me the paperwork. I could see that her name was Rouchelle.

"Please initial all the boxes marked with an X, then sign here and here," she instructed.

"Thank you," was all I could muster. I followed the directions, then pulled out my card for payment. She made her way back over to me, but this time, she politely smiled.

"I'm sorry," she said.

"Huh? What?" Had I incorrectly completed the paperwork? Did they not take credit cards?

"I'm sorry for being rude to you." I could see the other ladies leaning in our direction, likely trying to get within earshot of a possible altercation.

"I hadn't noticed," I said with a look of sarcasm.

"The first day you came to the office and I saw your surrogate, I just thought it was strange that your surrogate was white. We've had other surrogate arrangements, but the women are usually the same race. I felt that maybe you didn't think a black woman was good enough."

I went on to explain my situation. She was in awe even at the abridged version.

After explaining, she asked, "Can I give you a hug?"

I nodded. That day I made a new friend. Now it was time to see what was going on with Heidi.

Two weeks later, David and I arrived for the hospital tour. This wouldn't be the standard delivery, so I needed to confirm that the hospital was prepared.

The administrator, Lisa Todd, had already explained to us over the phone that Memorial was "surrogacy friendly." *Must be the new catchphrase*, I thought. We were just excited we'd finally meet our baby boy. David and I made our way to the fourth floor.

"We're here for the tour," David said once we reached the nurse's station.

"You must be the Gowdys," said Jean.

"Yes, we are," I said.

"Demetria will be right with you," she smiled. As we stood there waiting on the maternity floor, it felt like my oxygen was slowly dwindling. Standing on this floor felt surreal.

"Hello, Dr. and Mrs. Gowdy," a soft woman's voice uttered. Demetria, the hospital doula, was here to take us on our tour. The tour mainly consisted of directing David and me to a special holding area, set up for us and the members of our families.

"I had a chance to meet your surrogate earlier today," she said. I had wanted Heidi and me to do the tour together, but she seemed to make excuses every time I called. "This is the floor where she'll recuperate. The nurses will take great care of her," she continued.

As we walked the hall, we reaped the sounds that only a new baby can bring. We neared the end of the hall, and just as we made the turn, I took in a vision that arrested my heart. All sound had escaped me. I felt as if I were walking in slow motion. As we rounded the corner, I saw a single flower placed in the center of a door. Flashbacks rushed in. It became hard for me to catch my breath. I wanted to push open the door and boast that joy would come in the morning.

To say that David supported me was an understatement. I could feel his grip tighten. He'd heard my story a million times. My eyes welled up from the pain that I knew was behind that door.

"Excuse me, nurse! Can you give us a second?" David asked. Demetria politely moved out of earshot. "Hey, hey, are you okay?" David asked.

"I'll be fine. I just had a moment, and if I'm honest, I can tell you I may have many more. Yes, I've learned to be content in my barrenness, but that doesn't mean there won't be times when the disappointment, pain, and embarrassment won't be triggered."

I excused myself to the ladies room. "I can do all things because you strengthen me," I prayed. After a snotty nose check, eyeliner redo, and a touch of powder on my nose, this girl was ready to finish the tour.

Demetria took us to the waiting area where David and I would wait for our new arrival. Just knowing that we were this close made us smile with anticipation.

"So that concludes the tour," said Demetria. We thanked her as we made our way to the nearest elevator, down to the lobby, and off the maternity floor, at least for now.

## CHAPTER 27

# DON'T SHUT ME OUT

I'd hoped to see Heidi later in the week. We'd been gifted a 3D ultrasound by a doctor friend of David's. Unfortunately, my work schedule dictated an out-of-town trip. The doctor assured us that we'd receive a full-blown video of our little guy, but David would be there having all the fun in real time. It would make up for so many other appointments that he had to miss.

That night I spoke with David, and he gave me the biggest laugh.

"While Heidi and I watched the ultrasound, the technician pointed out that the baby had a lot of hair," he laughed. "Then Heidi says, 'Wow, I'm carrying a kid with an afro.'" David and I both had a good laugh. Things were moving fast; it was all smooth sailing from here. Well, not quite.

As David made his way downstairs, I was prepared to share some unbelievable news with him. As he walked closer to me, he was drawn in by the look on my face. I was anxious to let him know.

"David, Heidi's having triplets!" I paused.

"SHE'S WHAT!" he screamed.

"APRIL FOOL'S!" I shouted. David didn't find that funny at all. He was quite annoyed.

"Are you ready to go?" he asked.

"Yes, just let me pour the coffee in the mugs," I hurriedly said. We'd recently purchased a new SUV, as we knew we needed the space for Doc. It still had that new car smell that I loved. I hadn't had a new car in twelve years, so this was a much-needed upgrade.

When we arrived, Heidi and Dave were already sitting in the waiting room. It had been a month since I'd seen Heidi. She'd sent me pictures and videos since then. The contortions of her tummy looked almost alien, but beautiful, so I knew that Doc was growing leaps and bounds. But seeing her today, I couldn't believe just how much Doc had grown. She didn't look as if she'd gained much weight at all. The term "she's all baby" definitely had Heidi in mind.

The four of us gave our familiar greetings, but I could tell Heidi was distant. She didn't have much to say. I was hoping she wasn't regretting this labor of love. I remembered right after our last appointment, she seemed withdrawn; there was her solo hospital tour. Maybe it was just another bad day.

David and I sat in the waiting room while the exam took place.

"Dr. and Mrs. Gowdy, you can come back now," a nurse called. As we walked past the nurse's station, Rouchelle gave me a wink and a smile, and I returned the gesture.

"Everything looks good," said Dr. Hall. We hadn't seen him since the initial visit. He was all smiles and proud of how far we'd come. Heidi was still sitting on the table, and her David was standing by her side.

"We need to schedule the actual date of the delivery," Dr. Hall said. "I see Dr. Achebe wrote down the week of April 28. Have you all decided on a specific day? We need to get on the hospital's schedule for the surgery."

"What if the baby decides to come earlier?" Heidi's David asked.

"That could happen, and if it does, we'll make adjustments. Thirty-nine weeks is the magic number, so let's plan with that number in mind," Dr. Hall responded.

"Is there a possibility that I could have the baby naturally?" Heidi chimed. The room went silent.

"I don't think we ever considered a VBAC," said Dr. Hall.

"I thought the doctors had decided early on that you would have a C-section?" I reminded her.

"A vaginal birth after cesarean (VBAC) is not something that should be taken lightly," said Dr. Hall. He started sifting through his notes. He went on to explain the complications of this type of procedure. "I see back in the notes where this was discussed, but not recommended by Dr. Kidman. I, too, would not recommend this, considering the situation."

"What situation?" Heidi snapped.

"If this were your baby, we could certainly discuss this and I would likely vote against it, but in the end, the decision would be yours. Therefore, in this case, the Gowdys would have the final say."

"It's their baby, but my body," Heidi cried. I just stood there, dumbfounded.

"Heidi, as a medical professional, I'm not a fan of VBAC, especially since the previous cesarean was an emergency. It's just too risky."

Heidi looked at me. She could see the look of confusion on my face. I was dazed and confused, but David was downright salty.

"Look," said David. "We put in the contract that there would be a greater financial responsibility on our part for a C-section, and even a life insurance policy for your family should something unforeseen happen. It was never our goal to make you feel overlooked or slighted in any way. We've come too far for you to think otherwise."

"The last office visit that Kimberly and I had was when I thought about the VBAC. It wasn't even that I was against the C-section; it was just that no one showed any concern about what I would be going through. I felt dismissed," Heidi cried.

"I'm sorry, Heidi. Since we'd already talked about this early on, I didn't think there was anything to discuss," I whispered.

"I think we all want what's best for everyone involved, but a chance that my son could be at risk is a risk I'm not willing to take," David said.

The tears fell even faster from Heidi's face as she cried profusely. Her shoulders danced up and down as she heaved in and out, and her huge belly moved in unison. After David's matter-of-fact comments, I was sure we were in for a showdown and that Attorney Jackson would have to intervene.

"I'm so sorry, guys," Heidi said through tears. "I started thinking about the recovery time, then feeling dismissed. A little bit of it may even be hormones," she chuckled. "But I want to do what's best for your baby, so let's pick out a date," she said. The looks on all of our faces gave way to an exhale. We smiled from ear to ear.

I stepped forward to where Heidi sat. "Thank you, thank you so much." Our hug was warm and inviting. The next thing I knew, the Davids were hugging, and even Dr. Hall joined in on the lovefest. Once we all regained our composure, we finally came to a consensus. If all went as planned, on April 30, we were going to have a baby.

## CHAPTER 28

# FINAL TOUCHES

We only had a couple of weeks before the big day. Between work, life, and house-hunting for our dream home, we were burning the candle from both ends. We'd finally found a home we loved but had to delay the closing due to some constraints from the seller.

We had a million loose ends to tie up. For starters, the baby's room had to be perfect. My siblings and girlfriends wanted to host a baby shower, and it definitely would have cut down on all the out-of-pocket costs, but I decided against it, FOR NOW. I understood the logistics. My family was in Connecticut, and I had friends spread out throughout the East Coast. I knew how much sharing in my happiness meant to them, but I also knew how excited they would be to see my little one. That would mean another trip south. I thought it was best to kill two birds with one stone and have the shower shortly after the baby's birth, and since all the players would be in town, we could have the baby blessed the same weekend. That idea made perfect sense.

As for the baby's room, there had to be a theme.

I immediately thought of the onesie I'd given David to announce Doc's impending arrival. The onesie gave me the idea for a sports theme. We had the walls painted in Blue Cruise, which flowed nicely with the deep, rich espresso bedroom furniture. The crib, which was supposed to double as a toddler bed, along with a chest of drawers and changing table, fit nicely in the room.

Between the sports memorabilia that decorated the walls, we hung beautiful big block letters that spelled D A V I D. I knew that David wanted a namesake, as he's an only child, and he was clear about this from the beginning. I felt honored to name our son after his dad, the man who had changed my life. David was a strong name too. In the Bible, David is a king. Our son would likely not be a king, but I wouldn't rule out president.

The valances, handmade by Vapes, added that flare only she could bring. The monitor, piggy banks, mobile, teddy bears, plush throw rug, diaper pail, and glider all rounded out the room. While I handled the room, David had secured the car seats and put together the stroller and swing.

As David walked into the room, he said, "This looks nice. You did a great job."

"I'm glad you like it," I replied. Looking at the room, we were giddy. We both wore smiles from ear to ear.

"Now for the finishing touches. Stay right here, okay?" David said as he left the room. When he returned, he had in his possession a picture of a doctor holding a little boy on his lap. He'd always thought that represented him and his son. He wanted to hang it in the room. I loved the idea.

That suddenly gave me an idea of my own. "I'll be right back," I said. David knew exactly where I was going. Many years ago, while I carried Elijah, a friend gave me a picture of a woman cradling her newborn baby in her arms with the baby's head nestled into her bosom. I kept it tucked away, usually sitting in the back of my closet. I'd dreamt that one day, I'd cradle my baby in my arms the same way the artist depicted the woman on his canvas.

I retrieved it from the back of our closet, and we hung both pictures with care, both of us in tears. God was about to give us the desires of our hearts.

CHAPTER 29

# WE HAVE YOUR BACK

Weeks had turned into days, and in one week, I would be cradling my "snookums." Soon I would become a MOBY, Mommy Older Baby Younger, and I was ready.

A few other relatives had moved to Atlanta throughout the years. One was my mom's sister, Maisy. She moved from New York and was a ball of energy.

I had a hard time keeping up with her.

Tonight, she with our family and friends decided it was time to show a little love for David and me. After all, this was our last weekend before the baby. We freely agreed to have one last hurrah before the birth of our son. He was due to arrive on Tuesday, and our life of spontaneity was about to go out the window.

Earlier that day, I'd just finished an intense workout, so I was sweating profusely and in desperate need of a shower. The water was doing the trick. I decided to sit in the shower for a while to give myself some time to unwind from the workout.

*David should be home soon*, I thought to myself. He'd gone to the airport to pick up his parents. They were excited about joining tonight's festivities. Come Tuesday, they wanted to be the first to see their new grandson. Unfortunately, my parents couldn't make it until after his birth. The celebration started at 7:00 this evening, and it was already 2:00 p.m. Between the traffic and the amount of time it took me to get dressed, we were already late.

When I stepped out of the shower, I noticed that I'd received a text message. The text was from Heidi. It was a video, and from the still, I could see it was a baby bump pic. She was so good about keeping me in the loop. I planned to walk into my bedroom, put on some loungewear, then sit back and enjoy the show. I'd gotten as far as my undergarments, but the video was calling my name. I ran back into the bathroom, grabbed my cell, stood in the middle of the bathroom, and hit play. I could see my little guy moving around, not nearly as much as before, but I wasn't concerned. I knew that at this stage in the pregnancy, he was running out of room.

I noticed Heidi's hand instinctively rub her belly. At that moment, my reflection in the mirror caught my eye. My belly, my flat belly. The sight on the video and the sight in the mirror hit me. A wave of shame gripped my heart. The reality suckerpunched me in the face.

I'm broken. Why had this happened to me? I'm a good person. Of all the women in the world, David ended up with me. I was in a full-blown pity party.

"Save me, save me, Lord," I cried. In times like these, I knew of no one else. The tears were falling hard, and I heaved until I fell to the floor and curled up into a ball. "This isn't fair."

I'm the eldest of eight. Between my mom and dad, I have five siblings; my youngest two siblings were a result of my dad's second marriage to Debbie. As the eldest, I had been responsible for my younger siblings. I was a good aunt to their children, and a good godmother. How was it that I couldn't have kids? Over the years, I supported my sorors and friends, I'd celebrated their bundles of joy, even while dealing with my own pain.

"How does this make any sense?" The pain was raw. I held my belly as words like failure, loser, and barren flooded my mind. The bathroom sat above the garage, and I could hear its door opening. I had gotten so good at pretending that everything was okay. I knew I couldn't let my in-laws see me like this, but in that moment, my legs felt like lead pipes. They had traveled up for such an auspicious occasion, and at that moment, God's strength was made perfect in my weakness.

The beep of the door meant they were in the house. I crawled over to the vanity and practically scaled it so that I could stand. I ran into the closet and threw on my favorite kaftan, gathered the back of my hair up, and popped on a hair clip, then applied a few eyedrops. I was good as new.

"Sweetheart, are you upstairs?" yelled David.

"Yes, I'm on my way down," I replied. I cascaded down the stairs with a smile that could light up the night.

"Mom, Dad, it's so nice to see you," I greeted. David looked at me with a quizzical look. This guy knew me so well.

After reminiscing, laughing, and getting dressed, it was now close to 6:00 p.m. We had to be in Midtown by seven. I decided to go with a black jumpsuit and strappy, silver high-heeled sandals.

"David, can you help me with this bracelet?" I asked.

"Absolutely," he said. *You can never wear enough jewelry.* David pulled the car out of the garage and parked in the driveway. Parking in front of the door made it easier to help his parents get in the car. We were finally all belted in and ready to drive to Atlanta.

"Do you have change for the valet?" David asked. We rarely carried cash.

"I have cash," said Dad from the back seat.

The valet opened my door. "Thank you," I graciously said. As we made our way into the restaurant, the lighting was very dim, and the atmosphere felt kind of LA chic. A young woman greeted us with a pleasant smile, carrying a large menu in her arms.

"We're meeting friends. The name might be under Lipscomb or Galon." We weren't quite sure who set this up.

"Oh, yes. It's under Galon," she said. "Right this way." She directed us to a beautiful lounge just alongside the restaurant. It was already 7:30, so, hopefully, everyone had already arrived.

As soon as the door opened, Marvin shouted, "There they are!" Marvin's big mouth and big personality were on full display. We exchanged hugs with him and Geena and thanked them for getting us out of the house.

It was a room of about thirty people, and as we entered,

everyone turned in our direction. The group started clapping and cheering. It was surreal. I knew I would be on my feet toasting, laughing, and updating everyone, but first, I needed to find a nice, comfy spot for my in-laws. As we made our way over to a white leather sectional, I spotted the one person that I didn't think I'd ever see again, at least not at this function, and I certainly didn't want to talk to her.

David and I helped Mom and Dad with their jackets. "Would you like something to drink?" I asked them.

"Yes, I'll have a cab," Dad said.

"That goes for both of us," said Mom. No sooner than I turned to walk toward the bar, I heard my name.

"Kimberly!" I pretended not to hear her. "Kimberly!" She was now standing right next to me. I turned and found myself face to face with Halle. I hadn't seen her since her lecture about "crossing over," and I had no reason to talk to her.

"Halle, hi. I'm surprised to see you here." My irritation was showing.

"I called you a few times, I also left quite a few messages but didn't hear back from you," she uttered.

"I've been so busy, you know, with work, life, and crossing over," I couldn't help myself. Her eye contact left mine and looked to the floor. There was an uncomfortable pause.

"Kimberly, I just want to say I'm sorry. As soon as the words left my mouth, I knew I was wrong." She sounded sincere.

"I understand, but you have a right to your feelings, just as I have a right to cross over, as you called it." I was already ready to mingle with someone else.

"I no longer feel that way," she said. "I spoke with Janet, Geena, and your friend Vapes. Until you said it, I had no idea that you'd been working with surrogates for years, all of them black. I just assumed that Becky—"

"Heidi," I corrected her.

"Oh, sorry, Heidi. I assumed Heidi was your first choice," she finished.

"First of all, I said that at the table, and secondly, why does Heidi's race matter so much?" I asked. Before she could even answer, I continued. "I've had more than a few dumb comments about my decision. Somebody asked me if my son was going to be of mixed race. Another person asked me if my son was going to have her blood. Oh yeah, I think that was your husband, Troy. And someone else asked if he was going to look like David, Heidi, AND me. I even had a nurse tell me that she thought I chose Heidi because I thought black women weren't good enough." I chuckled.

"Look at how I slay every day, all day," I added. "And she thought I didn't think black women were good enough? Chile please."

By now, David and Troy had walked over to join us. I think my eye roll gave me away.

"What's going on over here?" David asked.

"Everything's fine," said Halle. "I just want to apologize to Kimberly and you, too, David, for my comment the last time we were together."

"Troy and I were talking about the same thing. No worries," said David.

"Like I just told David, I felt bad. I'm sorry," said Troy.

That night we made plans to reconnect at a later date, but right now I needed to get two glasses of cabernet.

My bubbly Aunt Maisy sashayed across the floor. "So, how's my favorite niece?" she asked. She always had a way of making me feel special.

"I'm doing great," I said.

"So, are you ready?" she asked.

"Yes. The room is finished, we got a new SUV, and I have more than enough clothes for this kid," I answered.

"I mean—"

"Excuse me, Auntie," I interrupted. "Can I get two glasses of the cab?" I ordered, then returned my attention to my aunt. "Sorry about that. What were you saying?"

"I mean, are you ready spiritually and mentally?" she asked.

"Yes, if it weren't for my relationship with God, I don't know that I'd still be here. I won't say there aren't times when I don't hurt, I had a moment earlier today, but after all I've been through, I'm stronger than ever." I smiled.

"Hey, Auntie, what's up?" My cousin Annette joined us. She leaned in and kissed Aunt Maisy.

"Mwah, how is my favorite niece?"

I rolled my eyes. I thought she just said I was her favorite niece.

"So, what time do you want us to be at the hospital on Tuesday?" Annette asked. I had asked Aunt Maisy and Annette to come to the hospital for the birth, but I didn't know quite what to expect. Still, I needed the support.

"If you can get there around ten o'clock, that would be great."

"Memorial, right?" asked Annette.

"Right," I said.

I spent the evening basking in all the love. The hugs were long and welcoming. Still, it was getting late. None of us were spring chickens, and it was time to pack it up.

David stood. "Everybody, Kimberly and I would like to thank you for coming out this evening. We certainly appreciate every one of you. The birth of our child will be an exciting time for us. I know I won't be able to call everyone on Tuesday, so look for a text from either Kimberly or me once our little guy makes his arrival." David got a little emotional at the end. The crowd clapped and cheered for us, everyone stood, and we made our way out the door and over to the valet.

"I had a great time tonight," said Mom.

"So did I," Dad chimed.

"I wasn't expecting so many people to attend. I was thinking twelve max," said David. "I think we've become the poster child for not giving up." We all laughed.

The drive home was smooth sailing. Just three more days.

## CHAPTER 30

# THIS IS THE DAY

I felt like a child on Christmas morning, but instead of waking up to a cool December day, I woke up to a beautiful, sunny Tuesday morning. No, I couldn't run downstairs and find my beautifully wrapped gift under the tree, but I knew my gift was scheduled to arrive today, April 30, and I planned to do my own wrapping, in my arms and with my love.

Of course, neither David nor I slept much last night. We both tossed and turned, then turned and tossed. We had come so far by faith, and today all the tears we'd cry would be tears of joy.

*Prayer is the best part of waking up*, I thought as I said, "Amen." Today, my cup of coffee was running a close second. "Thank you, Lord, for a good life and a good cup of coffee." My coffee maker had already started doing her thing.

As I made my way downstairs, I noticed that my father-in-law was already sitting in the living room. That wasn't as surprising as the fact that he was completely dressed. I looked at my phone; it was only six a.m.

"Good morning, Dad," I said as I leaned over and kissed him on the cheek.

"Good morning, dear," he said.

"Would you like some tea or coffee?" I asked.

"Coffee sounds good."

"I see you're dressed and ready to go," I said.

"Well, I wanted to make sure I looked my best for the cameras," he laughed. I had a soror whose family owned a studio. She and I spoke during one of our sorority meetings, which gave me a brilliant idea. I would have her and her crew come to the house to interview us before we left for the hospital. I wanted to tell the story from the start of the day until the birth of my son.

"Dad, you look great. Cream and sugar?" I asked.

"Yes, heavy on the sugar," he said. We both laughed. I admired my father-in-law. He came to this country as a child in 1931, leaving parents and eleven brothers and sisters behind. His parents had relatives in America who were childless. They hoped he would not only bless his Aunt Eunice but that he would have a chance at a better life. His name is signed at Ellis Island. After serving in a segregated military on a brickmason's salary, he would be responsible for helping most of his relatives come to America.

As he held his cup, I looked at his hands, the hands that knew hard work and a long life. Because of that, coupled with the fact that David's mom graduated in the '60s from Juilliard, I knew my son would come from good stock. My little David "Doc" Gowdy. He had some big shoes to fill.

David finally made his way downstairs. "Good morning, Dad. Wow, look at you looking all dapper at this time of the morning," David chuckled.

"Do you want some coffee, babe?" I asked.

"Yes, please," he responded. "So, what time is Jocelyn coming?" he asked.

"She's supposed to be here at ten," I answered.

"So, this is where the party is." It was my mother-in-law, Bernice. Even at eighty-plus years old, she had the most beautiful caramel complexion. I know we don't crack, but geez!

I planted a big kiss on her forehead. "I know you want coffee, right?" I confidently asked.

By now, David had taken out turkey sausage and eggs. I made the coffee for Mom, then pulled out the bagels. We may as well have a big breakfast. Who knew the next time we'd have a chance to eat? We sat and reminisced for about an hour before we decided to get dressed.

As I made my way up the steps, my cell rang. I thought to myself, *What took her so long?*

"Good morning, Mom," I said.

"Hey babe, I know you probably have a lot going on right now, but I wanted to let you know that I am praying for you, David, and the baby. I love you, sweetheart."

"Mom, as soon as the baby arrives, you will be the first to know." I blew her a kiss before we hung up. Unlike David's mom, my mom hadn't gone to college. What she lacked in formal education, she made up in common sense. She worked hard along with my dad to raise six daughters. Like all good parents, she wanted the best for us. She was a praying woman, and I learned what love looks like from her. I couldn't remember a time my mom wasn't there for me. I planned to model my parenting skills after her, minus the occasional switch.

After we finished dressing, we all congregated back in the kitchen. By now we had received numerous messages, mostly texts. The prayers, expressions of love, and well-wishes meant everything. As I sat there reading them, the doorbell rang.

"I'll get it," said David. I knew it had to be Jocelyn. As soon as he opened the door, I heard her voice.

"Hey, David!" she greeted. She reminded me of Jill Scott, very down to earth and sassy all at the same time. Then I heard a man's voice; it must have been her dad. The butterflies in my stomach had officially arrived.

My in-laws remained seated as I made my way to the front door. I noticed that three people had joined us.

"Hey Soror!" I gleefully said to Jocelyn.

"Hey Soror," she said with a warm, hearty embrace.

"Okay, I was introducing David to my dad," she said. "Dad, this is Kimberly. Kimberly, this is my dad, Clement." He greeted me with a warm hug.

"Hello, Mr. Clement." Even as an adult, I still prefaced an elder's name with Mr. or Miss. I could see a younger gentleman standing off to the side. He had a huge camera placed in the front of his feet. We made eye contact.

"Hello," I said.

"I'm so sorry, Kimberly. This is Darryl. He's the videographer. He used to work for MSNBC." We officially greeted each other. Now that all the players were here, it was lights, camera, action!

Darryl was a pro. He was moving things around in the living room to make the perfect setting.

"Even the smallest thing could ruin the perfect background," I heard him say. Mr. Clement had already started snapping pictures. My goal was for each of us to express what this day meant. I wanted our son to know that although I didn't carry him, he was wanted and loved.

"Okay, first I'd like to interview you as a family, then I'll ask you questions individually," Darryl instructed as he directed the four of us over to the couch. He looked into the lens to make sure things looked okay, then he angled the camera, crossing from left to right, capturing Dad first, then Mom, David, and last was me. I sat at the end of the sofa.

"So, tell me how you feel at this moment," Darryl said. We were each a little camera shy, but once we got started, the words of love just poured from each of us.

"Now for the individual interviews," Darryl announced. "First David and then Kimberly," he instructed. "David, I heard a little about your journey. Tell me what having a son at this stage in your life means."

"It means everything. I'm an only child. My dad is older, and I'm getting older. My dad did so much . . ." He started to cry.

"It's okay," I said.

"My dad did so much by helping his family come to this country. I want to leave a legacy, a namesake for him. I want to honor him. Our son's middle name will be Joshua. David Joshua Gowdy," he cried.

"What a strong name," Jocelyn shouted. I don't think there was a dry eye in the room at this point. I know mine certainly weren't.

"Okay, Kimberly, you're up," said Darryl.

"Oh, boy, let's get the tissue. She's already a basket case," David laughed. I knew I needed to get myself together. I wanted this video to be exciting, fun, and full of love. I had to focus on my inner Oprah. I ran into the powder room to check my eyes. I was sure to purchase a nice waterproof eyeliner after the incident during the hospital tour. I took my seat right in the middle of our tan leather sofa. I looked like I was preparing to give the news. Shoulders back, big inhale, then exhale. I waited for Darryl's cue in five, four, three, two, one.

"Kimberly, tell us what today means to you," he asked.

After a long pause, I said, "Today is the day I've waited for most of my adult life. Today represents an answered prayer. I just assumed that one day I'd get married, start a family, and live happily ever after. Things didn't work out that way," I said.

"What is it that you want your son to know?" Darryl asked next.

"I want him to know that he is one loved little boy, and that although I didn't carry him, the love that I feel for him is unconditional." My eyes welled. "I want him to know that, more than anything, I wanted him, that the uniqueness of his birth makes him special, and not one day went by that my heart didn't beat without the thought of him," I cried.

"I think we captured it," said Darryl. "Now I'd like for you all to just casually sit at the table and converse." He was certainly a professional. Jocelyn had outdone herself. Why didn't he catch us this morning? We had so much to say then.

As the camera rolled, we enjoyed small talk. Darryl walked about the house capturing our home from different angles.

"Hey Darryl, I would like for you to get some footage of my son's room," I said excitedly.

"Of course, that's a great idea," he said. I jumped up and

made my way upstairs. I couldn't wait to show off the baby's room. Jocelyn and Mr. Clement followed.

"I love the pictures," said Jocelyn. I was sure to explain the significance of the woman cradling the baby.

"That story warms my heart," said Mr. Clement.

"Darryl, will you be back on Friday?" I asked.

"Yes, Jocelyn said you wanted to capture footage of the baby once you bring him home," he responded.

"I would like a picture of me in this same pose, cradling my son," I sighed.

"Wow! That is going to be beautiful," said Jocelyn.

"We can also capture a picture of David and the baby." I pointed to the picture. "It may be a few years before he's as big as the kid in the pic, but the sentiment is still the same," I said.

"Kimberly, we need to get ready to leave for the hospital," David called from downstairs.

We were scheduled to arrive at 12:45 p.m. It was already 11:30 a.m., so we made our way downstairs. David was waiting for me at the bottom steps. Dad and Mom had already put on their jackets. Darryl packed up his equipment.

"David, I'd like to ride down with you and Kimberly, if that's okay?" Darryl asked.

"Sure," David said.

"I want to get footage of the ride to the hospital and the looks on your faces along the way," he said. This guy was on his game. When Jocelyn said she had me covered, I didn't realize just how much.

Before we exited the door, David led us in prayer. He prayed for the health of our son, for Heidi and Dave, and he thanked God in advance for answering our prayers.

CHAPTER 31

# THIS MOMENT

After packing up the car, we made our way down Georgia 400. Darryl kept the video rolling the entire time. I felt like I was on an episode of *The Real Housewives of Atlanta*.

Surprisingly, the traffic was light, which was pretty rare for this stretch of highway. Darryl was capturing highway signs for that added touch—Roswell, Sandy Springs, Buckhead, etc. Maybe he thought this footage would someday play at the Sundance Film Festival.

I looked over at David as he intently watched the road. I could only imagine what he was feeling. For me, it was the butterflies. They danced around in my stomach at full throttle.

"Are you doing okay?" David asked.

"I guess so," I replied. The truth is, I was scared. Just then, the phone rang. It was my Aunt Maisy.

"Hello sweetheart, are you on your way?" she asked. Everyone could hear her voice through the car's speakers.

"Yes, Auntie," I answered.

"Well, I should be there any minute," she said. I could always count on her. Since my mom couldn't be there, my aunt had stepped up to the plate. Like so many, she had witnessed my journey and seen my anguish. I knew more than anything that she wanted this for David and me.

"I'll be there in about fifteen minutes," I said.

"Sweetheart, I just want you to know that I love you, and everything will be fine," she sighed.

"Thank you, Auntie. You always know what to say. I'll see you in few minutes," I said.

"Hello, Maisy," my mother-in-law shouted from the back seat. After a brief conversation between my Aunt Maisy and my in-laws, we all said our goodbyes. Ten minutes later, we made our turn onto the hospital grounds.

"Dad and Mom, we'll drop you off in front," David said. Once the car stopped, I could see my cousin Annette standing with Aunt Maisy in front of the hospital. I waved feverishly at the two of them. They both walked over to help my in-laws out of the SUV. Darryl decided to join them.

"I'd like to capture some footage as the two of you are walking toward the hospital," he said.

"Okay," we agreed. Jocelyn and Mr. Clement had parked and were now making their way toward the front of the hospital while David and I parked the car.

"Are you ready?" he asked. I looked into his eyes, then put my hand on his face.

"I love you so much, and I don't know what I would do without you. I'm ready, but only because you're here with me," I said. He leaned over and kissed me.

"If I had to choose anyone to take this journey with, it would be you," he said. In the words of Mary, it was now time to go get our blessing.

As we made our way to the front of the hospital, I could see Darryl and Mr. Clement capturing footage and snapping photos. I felt like a celebrity. The warm embrace of Aunt Maisy and Annette was interrupted by a nurse who'd come outside looking for David and me. We were told to arrive in the lobby area at 12:45, but it was only 12:30, so I knew we weren't late.

"Hello, is this the Gowdy family?" a tall brunette asked.

"Yes, I'm Kimberly Gowdy," I said.

"It's so nice to meet you," she said with a bubbly tone. "I'm Ann."

"Is everything okay?" David asked.

"Yes, I'm here to escort you into the waiting area," she said. Mr. Clement was still snapping pictures. "Would you mind if we took a few more pics outside?" Darryl asked.

"By all means, there's no rush," she said. Mr. Clement snapped a shot of Nurse Ann. At that point, she willingly joined our photoshoot. I was smiling on the outside, but on the inside, the adrenaline rush was real.

After about ten minutes, Nurse Ann chimed in. "I think we'd better head up now," she directed. At that point, everyone made way for David and me to walk up front.

As I walked alongside Nurse Ann, she whispered, "We've all been briefed on your situation." She smiled, and I smiled back. We reached a small waiting area when she stopped. "We have this separate waiting room right here for your family," she said. "Because of the nature of the birth, the hospital will allow the cameras to come back," she said.

At that point, my in-laws, aunt, and cousin got in one last hug.

"We'll all be thinking of you," said Dad. Surrogacy wasn't an ideal situation, but it was mine. I had come to fully accept my inadequacy. No, I couldn't carry a child, but what I could do was be the best mom I could to Doc. The tears had already started streaming from everyone's eyes. I knew today would be filled with tears; I just didn't think it would be this soon.

"I'll stay back with the family," said Mr. Clement. We nodded.

Looking at the tears in my eyes, Nurse Ann whispered, "Are you ready?"

"Yes," I said. She led the way as we followed. Just after we made it through the double doors, she stopped.

"We're going to have you sit in here," she said. She opened the door, and we followed her inside. The room was quaint. There were two chairs placed in the center.

A bathroom was to my right, and on my left, lined up against the wall, was a contraption of which I had no familiarity along with a scale. She could see the look of curiosity on our faces.

"Once the baby is born, we'll bring him back to this room," she explained. "Another nurse or I will wash and dress him on this table. The lights above will keep him warm. We'll weigh him in here as well. That way you can spend as much time as possible with him."

"Thank you so much. What a blessing," I cried.

"The first thing I'll need is for both of you to change into these gowns," she said.

"Why?" I asked.

"You need to kangaroo with the baby once the baby is born," she responded. She could see the look on my face, so she explained further. "It's important that the baby has skin-to-skin contact with you."

I wasn't prepared for this, but suddenly I felt like a participant in the birth of my child, and boy did I feel good. I walked into the bathroom, out of camera shot, to put on the gown. Jocelyn and Darryl were still filming. By the time I returned, David had already changed.

"I'm going to let everyone know you're here," Nurse Ann said. Before she walked out of the room, she turned to us and said, "I know it's easier said than done, but try to relax. As I said earlier, everyone has been briefed on this situation, so you're in good hands." She smiled. I gave her a warm embrace. I needed every bit of encouragement I could get.

Once she left the room, Jocelyn and Darryl chose to find a spot on the floor. We all needed to save our energy for the main event. David and I sat in the chairs.

"I wonder what's going on with Heidi," I said. David could see that I was full of nervous energy.

"I'm sure they'll tell us something soon. Don't worry," he assured me.

The door swung open, and a petite nurse with long brown hair excitedly entered the room.

"Hello! You're the Gowdys, I presume?" She sounded like she was out of breath.

"Yes," we said.

"I'm Brittney." She was practically jumping out of her skin. "Okay, so, everything is fine. Heidi is on her way to the operating room," she exhaled. "As soon as I know more, I'll let you know," she finished.

"Thank you so much," I whispered.

"You're soooo welcome! I've never been a part of a surrogacy birth, so as you can see, I'm a little excited," she said.

"No, we hadn't noticed," said David. We all laughed. Somehow Brittney had managed to lighten up the mood, but as soon as she left the room, the quiet gave way to a wave of emotions. David started pacing the room while I rocked back and forth in my chair. We each looked like we were more ready for a straitjacket than a baby.

It had been forty-five minutes and still no news. David sat down and held my hands.

"I think we need to pray," he suggested. "Father, we thank you for—" The door flew open. It was Nurse Brittney, and she was grinning from ear to ear.

"Congratulations!" she squealed.

"She had the baby?" I asked nervously.

"YES! The baby is here! I saw him, and he's beautiful." David and I leapt to our feet, crying and laughing all at the same time.

"Congratulations," said Jocelyn and Darryl. The room was electric. We just assumed we'd have to sit and wait a little while longer to see our angel, but Nurse Brittney was full of surprises.

"I want you all to follow me," she said. "You've waited long enough." I clutched my shaking hands to my face. David and I followed her with Darryl and Jocelyn on our heels. The double doors, meant only for hospital staff, opened. As we made our way around the corner, we saw doctors and nurses congregating at the end of a corridor. They all turned and looked at David and me. Nurse Brittney positioned us on the opposite side of the corridor.

As we waited, we noticed a man walking down the hall. As

he got closer, we realized it was Heidi's David. No sooner than we recognized his face, we were startled by the most beautiful, angelic sound of all. The sound of a newborn baby's cry echoed down the hall as we cast our gaze on a tall, slender nurse wheeling a bassinet in our direction.

"David, it's the baby!" I cried. He wrapped his arm around my shoulder and pulled me in close. I could see Darryl's camera taking in the moment behind the lens. That moment, my moment, had finally come.

Like the consummate gentleman, Heidi's David stepped aside and allowed the bassinet to take center stage. The approaching bassinet was in real time, but the moment felt surreal. As the cries grew closer, the noise level among the crowd got louder. By now, we could see the huge smile on the nurse's face. It was Nurse Ann.

Just before she reached us, we heard her say, "Congratulations! You have a son."

My gaze shifted down and I laid eyes on the most beautiful thing I'd ever seen. But I froze. It was David who took control of the situation. With tears flowing from his eyes, he reached into the bassinet and caressed our baby.

"Wow, I have a son," he cried. Although I had waited for this moment, it just didn't seem real. I could hear the cheers and the applause, I could see Darryl's camera rolling, but the only words that escaped my lips were, "I'm a mom? I'm a mom?" I asked. I was in disbelief.

The baby was still wailing at full capacity. "Let's take him to the room," suggested Nurse Ann. We made our way back to the room.

"I need you to sit here and open your gown," Nurse Ann directed. I remembered the cameras, so I discreetly followed instructions. The nurse picked up my screaming baby and placed him onto my chest. The moment his skin touched mine, the crying stopped. It was magical.

I wrapped his shivering body inside my gown. The love I felt for this little person was like no other. To think that I almost missed out on one of life's greatest gifts brought fresh tears to my eyes.

Darryl captured my quieting skills on video. He sent the footage over to my family with the title, "This tender moment just happened." David watched over me and his son with a keen eye, but I knew he was longing for his turn. I was so afraid of standing and passing him to David, so I asked for help.

"Nurse, would you mind handing him over to his dad?" I asked. She was a pro as she gently but efficiently removed him from my arms and handed him to his dad.

"This feels unbelievable," said David. Our little guy was safe in his father's arms. I knew that feeling. Every day I find safety in my Father's arms. I knew after seeing Darryl's video, our families were bursting at the seams to meet this little guy.

By now, Nurse Brittney and Nurse Ann were preparing the room.

"We need to weigh him," one of them said. The nurse had to practically tear him out of David's arms. Eight pounds, three ounces, and twenty-one inches long.

"He's a little chunk," said Nurse Ann. "I think five pounds of it is his hair." We all laughed.

"Can we have my parents come back to see him?" asked David.

"I think I can arrange that," said Nurse Ann. "But first we need to get him cleaned up," she suggested. As we watched his first bath, Darryl and Jocelyn continued to capture everything. I was so caught up in the moment that I'd almost forgotten they were there. We were sending text messages and pics of our little guy as the "congratulations," "atta boy," and "we love you" messages kept coming.

After Doc was looking good, sporting a diaper, T-shirt, cute little hat, and swaddled in the standard white, blue, and pink blanket, it was time for him to make an appearance. Nurse Ann left the room. As I waited for his grandparents to come, I took that moment to thank God.

As I sat in the chair holding my baby close, I studied his face and held his cheek next to mine. His soft skin felt like a dream. My tears fell atop his head, but this time, they were tears of joy. When Nurse Ann returned, she had surprised us by bringing the entire crew to the room. The noise level rose tremendously, and the hugs ensued.

After we seated my father-in-law, I stood and gently placed his grandson in his arms. David stood over his shoulder, and the room took in three generations of Gowdys. My mother-in-law held him next. She started singing him a soft lullaby, and it was the sweetest sound.

Once Doc was back in my arms, I didn't want to let him go. Aunt Maisy and Cousin Annette patiently waited for their turn.

"I think he's a little tired. I'd better hang on to him for a while," I said. They laughed. They knew I had already become a mama bear. There was a knock at the door, and an older black woman dressed in a blue suit and glasses walked into the room.

"Hello." She looked around the room wearing a big smile. We all greeted her. She looked at me since I was holding the baby, assuming I must be the new mom. "Are you Kimberly?" she asked.

"Yes," I answered.

"I'm Lisa Todd, the hospital administrator," she beamed.

"Oh my goodness," I smiled. I'd spoken with her several times around the time of the hospital tour, as she was responsible for setting up the room for David and me and assigning the nurses. I stood and handed the baby to David. "It is so nice to put a face with the name," I said. She agreed. David also expressed his appreciation.

"Well, I have one more surprise for you," she said.

"We already have our biggest surprise. Are you going to tell me there's another baby?" David joked.

"Nothing like that," she laughed. "I know you all inquired about staying overnight. At the time, we didn't have a process in place, but I wanted to extend that option to you." She smiled.

We were overjoyed. The thought of having to leave the baby at the hospital was the one thing that we dreaded.

"Thank you so much!" we said.

"The stay will be our gift to you, so there's no charge," she said excitedly. After all the expenses for surrogacy, that was music to our ears.

"Free? We haven't heard the word free in years," I said.

For the next hour, the room filled with spontaneous visits from hospital staff, phone calls, text messages, and selfies. We were going to be moved upstairs shortly, but during all the commotion, David and I had spoken with Nurse Ann about another visit. She walked into the room and asked us to come with her. Doc was fast asleep in his bassinet.

As we walked down the hallway, we stopped just in front of a curtained-off room. Nurse Ann politely asked the occupant if we could come in.

"Yes," was the response and we entered the room.

"There she is," I whispered. Heidi was lying in the bed with her David standing over her.

"I'll leave you alone," said Nurse Ann. David and I walked over and stood on the opposite side. It seemed like only yesterday that the four of us stood in this same position as a five-day-old embryo, who would become Doc, found comfort in her womb. I knew she was tired, but as bad as I knew she felt, I could only wish I experienced what she was feeling. My hand reached for hers, and I held it softly.

"Thank you for what you did for us. My life is forever changed because of you," I said. I also thanked Dave for agreeing to take this journey with us. David expressed his gratitude to them as well.

Nurse Ann returned. "I have someone here who would like to get a photo of the four of you," she said. Darryl walked in with the biggest grin.

"I just wanted to get a few casual pics, and then I'm out," he said. We knew Heidi was still out of it, but she was a trooper and agreed to the photos. We continued our conversation and tried to pretend he wasn't there. I told her that I'd be staying in the hospital that evening. She knew how much that meant to me. Here she was, the one in all the pain, and yet she was still excited about my happiness. I kissed her forehead and hugged Dave. The Davids shook hands as if we'd just closed on a house, but I knew we were all thankful for the way things turned out.

It had been a long day. We made our way upstairs to our room for the night. I hadn't planned on staying overnight, so the hospital gown that I was still wearing would have to do. By now, everyone was tired and hungry.

"Are we still going out to celebrate?" asked Aunt Maisy. "I'm starved."

"So am I," Annette added.

"I think we need to go somewhere and have a celebratory toast," said Dad. David was completely on board.

My aunt had to help me with Doc's first diaper change. It was something about the look of his navel in a clip that made it impossible. I did manage to swaddle our son as best I could. Swaddling seemed so easy when we practiced on the doll, but with the constant squirming of a real child, not so much. I fed Doc his bottle, no more than six ounces. Soon, he was fast asleep.

By then, everyone was getting restless. Food had become a necessity, and we previously planned to meet up with friends after the baby. After all, we thought we were leaving our baby at the hospital. I called the nurse's station and asked for the nurse on call to come to our room. Once she arrived, I laid out our plans.

"We're going out to celebrate the birth of our son," I said. She looked at me with a very curious look on her face.

"Oh," she paused. "As long as someone will still be here with him, then that's fine," she expressed. I froze. Her words, although polite, hit hard. For my entire adult life, I had been able to come and go as I pleased. I had never really been solely responsible for anyone except myself. I was now responsible for another human being. Doc needed someone to stay with him, and that someone was me.

"I'm sorry, I don't know what I was thinking," I said.

"Oh, don't feel bad." She smiled.

"It's just that, um, oh, we weren't supposed to be staying overnight," I was babbling. My Aunt Maisy had witnessed the exchange. I looked at her. "I'm someone's mom," I said.

"You are indeed." She smiled. Everyone gathered their things to go, including David. "I'll drop off Mom and Dad then head back," said David. I knew that would be after the lobster and champagne dinner, but I was getting the better end of the deal.

Once everyone left, I walked over and knelt next to the bassinet and watched my newborn sleep.

Later that night, I sat in bed, waiting for David to return. I already had the recliner set up for him. As I lay there, I heard a knock at the door; it was the on-call nurse. She brought me a gift from Heidi. The gift was on ice. This angel of a woman took the time to send me colostrum. Heidi truly was a twenty-first-century wet nurse. My eyes filled with tears.

As Doc suckled, I thought of all the other times I'd been in this position. I was sitting in a hospital bed, crying over my baby just like tonight, but this time, they were tears of joy. This time, I had my baby, and the one thing I didn't have was a white flower on my door.

CHAPTER 32

# THE ADJUSTMENT

The moment we left the hospital, we were filled with joy and anxiety. I knew I was ready, but bouts of nervousness started to kick in. My mind had just gone through nine months of praying for our baby to make it into my arms, but a whole new set of fears arose.

Before we left the hospital, David and I decided to have him circumcised. Dr. Achebe, who delivered him, also performed the procedure. In the words of Attorney Jackson, "Having the Pre-Birth Order in place makes all the difference." We were able to make all decisions about the birth of our child, including this procedure.

I sat in the back of the SUV with Doc in his rear-facing car seat, as we were instructed, looking at his perfect skin. When we pulled into our driveway, I could see a big balloon tied to our door that read, "It's a Boy." I didn't know who the culprit was, but it sure made me feel good. My in-laws greeted us in a normal fashion, but they quickly averted their attention toward the baby.

That first month was tough. I got more sleep when I was pledging into my sorority than I got taking care of my baby. David's ex-wife, Diana, brought us some of our favorite Jamaican fare, and his daughters, Angela and Gabrielle, came over to welcome their little brother into the family. David's cousin, Dr. Pearl, and her husband, who was also a doctor, were asked to be his godparents, along with my sister Shane and her husband, Darnell. Having godparents on both sides, we knew we had him covered.

I also called and checked on Heidi a few times. I couldn't forget the physical pain she must have still been experiencing. It was so nice to hear her voice. Of course, I thanked her a million more times.

My family and friends had already made plans for my baby shower in the coming months since most of them would be coming from long distances. I told Heidi that it was a must that she attend. She agreed. The good news was that we could cover all the bases in the same weekend—the baby shower, Doc's blessing, and a speech that I intended to share with all those who had come along with me on this journey. The bad news was that David and I were also scheduled to move into our dream home just before the shower. The stress of a new baby coupled with the stress of moving, all within three months, was nuts. We hadn't thought it through.

One week after the birth my soror, Jocelyn, and her photography crew were scheduled to come back to our home to take additional pictures. It had taken everything in me to get myself together. My hair hadn't seen a comb all week, and finding time to shower was rare, but somehow we pulled it off.

The doorbell rang. "Kimberly, can you get the door?" David asked. These days, David and I were both so tired, we were begging the other to go the extra mile. Get the door. Get the bottle. Change the diaper. But somehow, I was always the one going the distance.

Thank God my in-laws were still with us. At eighty-seven, my father-in-law wasn't a hands-on helper, but seeing the happiness on his face excited me even more than my vat of coffee in the morning. It helped me to endure. My mother-in-law was always good for a few lullabies to get the baby off to sleep. Then there was my family, who called a million times. I appreciated the love, I needed the love, but I also needed sleep. I was told to sleep when the baby sleeps. That was great, but at two o'clock in the morning, I wanted to sleep, but he did not.

I made my way to the door. "Hey, Soror. Hey, Darryl. Long

time no see." We all laughed. I noticed Mr. Clement was not with them.

"Hey Jocelyn, where's your dad?" I asked.

"Since we're only doing photos and no video, we just needed the two of us." My father-in-law made his way downstairs and smiled at the familiar faces.

I ushered Jocelyn and Darryl inside. "Well, before you take one photo, can you please let a sistah put some lipstick on?" I asked.

As I ran upstairs to make some finishing touches on my make-up, David was coming downstairs.

"Hey, guys. What's up?" I heard David say. When I reached the loft area upstairs, I could hear my mother-in-law singing a sweet song to my cherub. She had such a way with him. I was thankful we had one more week to enjoy their presence.

"Mom, they're here. I need a minute to get my lipstick, then I'll take the baby off your hands," I said.

"Take your time, dear. I could get used to this." She smiled. As I looked at the pure joy my little guy brought to his grandmother, I wanted to capture it.

I called out from the loft, "Jocelyn, I'd like a few shots of these two upstairs, so let's start in the loft." I could hear the footsteps making their way up. As Jocelyn reached the top, my eyes directed her to the scene taking place on the sofa.

"I'll be right back. I'm sure you can take it from here," I said. As I walked into the master bedroom, I could hear the rendition of oohs and ahhs. They must've been enjoying that scene just as much as I did. After a little lip color, powder, and a quick once-over, I was ready for the camera.

As I walked back toward the loft, I could hear Darryl giving instructions. "Okay, tilt your head slightly left." When I walked into the room, I could see the smiles on David and Dad's faces. What a sight.

For the next couple of hours or so, we posed, we laughed, and we even cried. The real tearjerker came when it was time for

David and me to pose like the pictures in the frames. David positioned Doc in his right arm. The child in the photo was more of a toddler, but the sentiment was the same. Once in position, he stared lovingly at our sleeping infant. The moment was captured perfectly. I could see a tear roll down David's face. He was beyond in love with his namesake. Now it was my turn. David gently placed our son into my arms.

"Watch his head," I snapped. David gave his famous eye roll as he carefully handed him to me. I had waited for this moment, my moment, to feel the love I saw on the woman's face. It was an easy capture. I knew from the moment I placed Doc's head on my bosom and wrapped my arms around him that the love I had for this baby was like no other love I'd known. I loved my husband dearly, but this was different. This love came with a natural need to protect, like a mama bear protecting her cubs, and I could finally act on these feelings rather than imagining what could have been.

My mind flashed back to Elijah, but at that moment, I realized my heart was big enough to love them both. His memory would always be with me. From this moment, I would prayerfully experience the love, the trials, the ups and downs, and the pride of watching our son grow into manhood, all while keeping Elijah's memory in my heart.

My heart was full. God had poured me out a blessing that I didn't have room enough to receive.

## CHAPTER 33

# MOVE-IN DAY

"Be careful with that armoire," David directed. It was moving day, and it was rough. Between the two of us, we didn't realize just how much we'd acquired. Add in all the baby things along with sleep deprivation, and you've got a recipe for short tempers all the way around. I'd lovingly started calling David "Mood" since I wasn't sure what mood he'd be in each day.

Before moving into our new home, David and I had Doc's room painted with the same beautiful blue as before, but this time we added beautiful billowy clouds that adorned the ceiling. This room was even more precious than the last. A nice touch was the bedroom came with its own bath, which made it easy to rinse off pacifiers and bathe him all without having to leave the room.

By now, Miss Loretta, the nanny we'd met through David's colleague, had made her way into our hearts. She certainly knew how to care for a baby, and that helped us catch up on some much-needed rest. I'd started working again, but only from home. The thought of leaving my baby boy took some weaning. I'd eventually get there, maybe in about five years.

Dr. Pearl, Vapes, Janet, Shane, and Soror Ciera were all working with my family and friends to finalize the shower. I was skeptical about moving the same week as the shower, but my girls assured me that all I needed to do was show up. David and I had not let anyone outside of the family and very close friends see our baby. The only time he'd been out of our home was for doctor's visits and a photo shoot with his siblings, Angela and

Gabrielle. The girls wanted to present a photo album to their dad for Father's Day. David was right when he said they would come around.

The debut of our son needed to be on our time. We'd heard too many comments, and had to defend our decision too many times—not to most, but just the ignorant. Since the shower was swiftly approaching, we chose that occasion for our three-month-old to make his brief public debut. I knew the house wouldn't be perfect, but my family wasn't here to see my home. Their attention was solely on meeting the new addition to our family. My colleague Chidima had also blessed us just as she said, and we had an African naming ceremony. Doc's African name was Chinua, which means God's blessing, a meaning that couldn't be more perfect.

It was just two days until the baby shower, and a few of my sorors had flown in. They arrived early to get things in order. If we were celebrating a baby girl, the favors would have been full of pink and green, but instead, baby blue and other muted colors would have to do.

My dad was also scheduled to arrive today. David had already made the trek to the airport to pick him up, so I knew it was just a matter of time before I saw him. I was an absolute daddy's girl. It might sound a little cliché, but my dad has always been my hero. He and my mom married young and had six daughters, most of us very close in age, but that didn't stop him from working to provide the best for his family. I watched him move up the ranks within the same company, and he retired just short of fifty years. He believed in a man taking care of his family, and that was also one of the qualities I loved most about David.

"Kimberly, I think David's back," Ciera, my soror, shouted. She and the girls were in the process of putting favors together. I secured Doc in his swing, and walked over to the door with anticipation to greet my dad. The door opened, and there stood a handsome man smiling at me with arms wide open.

"Daddy!" I gave him the biggest hug.

"Hello, baby girl. It's so good to see you." Tears of joy fell from my eyes. It didn't take long before he started looking around. "Where's the baby?" he asked. I walked over to the swing. My dad followed. He reached for his grandson the moment he saw him.

I didn't want to interrupt the moment, but I did. "Dad, I'll take him out for you. That will give you time to wash your hands," I suggested.

"I get the hint," he laughed. He knew I was a mom protecting her cub.

CHAPTER 34

# SHOWER ME WITH YOUR LOVE

It was the day before the shower. Any minute now, we'd receive a call alerting us that someone was at the gate. David and Dad were talking in the kitchen. Miss Loretta and I were upstairs in the baby's room. My sorority sisters weren't expected back until that evening.

"Hello, precious baby," I cooed.

"I think he'll look adorable in this," said Miss Loretta, holding up a blue-and-white jumper. We were right in the middle of dressing Doc when the phone rang. I braced myself. Miss Loretta continued getting the baby dressed.

"Kimberly, they're here!" David yelled from downstairs. I did a quick check to make sure Miss Loretta had things covered. I ran downstairs as my heart raced and looked outside to see cars pulling into the driveway.

I knew my mom and sisters had made the trip, but as I continued to watch I saw nieces, nephews, and cousins exit their cars. I was overwhelmed with joy.

As they walked toward the house, I noticed that everyone made way for my mom to take the lead. As soon as I saw her take the first step up, I immediately opened the door.

"Mom!" I joyfully screamed. I was hugging the one person who had a front-row seat from the beginning of my quest for motherhood, who sat up with me at two o'clock in the morning and let me cry, and who endured with me when the pain seemed too hard to bear. But most of all, she was the one who took the time to pray for me. We stood locked in an embrace for what seemed like hours. I could feel family members patting my back as they stepped around us to go into the house.

"I am so happy for you, baby," she cried. We turned and walked into the house. Inside, my family was having a lovefest of their own with David and Dad. My mom and I joined in.

"Where's the baby?" everybody was asking.

"Miss Loretta is dressing him. I'll go up and get him," I said. With David on my heels, we started up the stairs.

David paused. "Oh, please make sure you wash your hands," he said. Spoken like a proud papa. About five minutes later, Miss Loretta joined David and me as we carried the portable bassinet downstairs. Everyone was leaning in to take a peek, but I was careful to cover his face with a blanket. David sat the bassinet on the living room coffee table, then slid the blanket from his face. There was an eruption of voices.

"He's beautiful." "What a beautiful baby." "Look at all that beautiful hair." Those were just some of the superlatives spoken about our baby. I bent over and picked him up.

"Give me that baby," said my mom. I gladly placed him in her arms. The joy on my mom's face said it all. Once we came down from the baby high, I introduced Miss Loretta; she was an immediate hit. Later on that day, David and Dad drove to the airport to pick up my in-laws; all of the family was officially here. The rest of the day was full of good food, laughter, and love.

Finally, it was the day of the shower. It started at two o'clock at a hotel in the Perimeter. The atmosphere of the house was crazy. That's what happens when you have eighteen people all under one roof. I insisted that all my family members stay with us. I knew I only had them for the weekend, and I wanted to enjoy every moment.

Miss Loretta and her husband, Mr. Charles, decided to meet

us at the venue, which meant my sisters came in handy with getting the baby ready. Once we reached the hotel, the butterflies in my stomach were in overdrive. It was the anticipation of seeing Heidi coupled with coming face to face with my naysayers regarding her race. I was almost shaking.

As soon as I stepped into the hotel, I saw Miss Loretta and Mr. Charles seated on a beautiful seat just outside of the banquet hall. The plan was for us to wait in a private room until the party started. Miss Loretta quickly retrieved the baby carrier and led me to the designated area. My family continued into the banquet hall. I wanted to make a grand entrance.

My sister Shane, who was also involved in the planning, alerted Vapes and Janet of our arrival. They both excitedly came over to greet me.

"Girl, I'm glad you're here. It looks like most of your guests have arrived," said Vapes.

"So, how do you want to do this?" Janet asked.

"David and I will make our entrance, mingle with our guests, and then in about ten minutes, we'll come back out here and scoop up Doc, Mr. Charles, and Miss Loretta," I said.

"Heidi is here," Vapes said excitedly.

"How do you know?" I asked.

"She was one of the first people to arrive. She introduced herself to me," said Vapes. "She's here with her husband."

"It's going to be nice for her to *really* see Doc for the first time," I said. Now that the plan was in place, it was show time.

"Miss Loretta, I'll be back in about ten minutes, then you can join the party, okay?"

"I'll be right here," she said. David and I followed Vapes and Janet.

"Stand out here for a minute," Vapes whispered. She and Janet made their way back into the venue.

"May I have your attention, please?" Janet shouted. "Without further ado, let's give it up for David and Kimberly!"

I could hear the applause as David and I entered the party. As

I looked around the room, I could see the familiar faces of our friends and family smiling and looking genuinely happy for us. There were round tables that sat eight in the center of the room and rectangular tables along the perimeter of the room, some covered in food and the others covered with gifts. Balloons decorated the room, and a huge "Congratulations" sign hung in the center of the wall. We initially stood in the front of the room and took in the cheers.

"Thank you all so much for coming," David said. We started to make our way around the room to greet people. The decorations and the food looked amazing. My girls had outdone themselves.

With each congratulatory hug, I received the same question: "Where's the baby?" I slyly smiled, and moved on to the next guest. My eyes finally landed on the one person I'd been looking for since I made my entrance. Heidi and Dave were sitting toward the back of the room. I immediately made my way over to them.

In the past forty-eight hours, I had been blessed with two of the most heartwarming hugs—first my mom, and now Heidi. Seeing her felt amazing and awkward all at the same time. I kept thinking to myself, *This woman carried my child.* I signaled for David to come back.

"Heidi, I have someone I want you to meet," I said.

"I think I know who it is," she replied. I told her that Doc would be here. Initially, I was going to have her meet him privately, but I decided to make their introduction public. The rest of the room was eating, chatting, and laughing as the hosts were setting up for games. Before we got into the heart of the party, I knew it was time for the guest of honor to make an appearance. I noticed all the hostesses congregated at the front of the room.

David and I made our way over to them. "We're going to get Doc," I said. Shane was responsible for the introduction, and she was ready. David and I discreetly left the room. Miss Loretta and Mr. Charles met us with enthusiasm as they placed Doc into David's arms.

As we made our way back to the room, I felt like I was moving in slow motion. Shane greeted us outside the room.

"Are you ready?" she asked. David and I nodded. "May I have your attention please." She repeated the request a couple of times. "For many years, I've watched my sister Kimberly endure the pain, hurt, and humiliation in her quest to become a mother. My sister has seven siblings, me being one of them, who all know the joys of parenting, yet not a single time did she ever show resentment or bitterness. She cheered for us and celebrated in our joys. I can't think of a better person who deserves this day more than her." We both began to cry as she spoke, both no longer able to hold back the tears.

Dr. Pearl took the mic. "Hello, everyone. I'm here to talk about my cousin, David. As an only child, my cousin has always wanted to have a namesake, a legacy. His daughters are the apple of his eye, but carrying on the Gowdy name was a desire that he shared with only a few. He and my Uncle Josh have always sacrificed for the Gowdy family, and I can't think of anyone who deserves this more," she cried. "There are a lot of gifts on the table, but Kimberly and David would like you to meet one of their greatest gifts. Please welcome DAVID JOSHUA GOWDY," she announced.

David and I made our way into the room amid the applause. As we walked into the room, David took a cue out of a scene from the movie *Roots*, and he held Doc up for all to see. Tears and cheers echoed from the crowd, but the only person I watched was Heidi.

After the applause subsided, David began to speak. "This is our son, David Gowdy. A friend has already given him his African name, Chinua, which means God's blessing, and every day, I am in awe of just how much God has blessed us. This child has brought tremendous joy to our lives. There have been those who have been curious about his appearance and/or questioned our judgment, but I can assure you that our son represents Kimberly and me 100 percent, and that, given the opportunity to do it again, we wouldn't change a thing," he said.

The crowd applauded his words, and I could hear a few people shouting, "Amen." It was my turn. I exhaled before I took the mic.

"Thank you all for coming to celebrate with us. I appreciate everyone being here, but there is one person that I would like to thank personally. Without her, none of this would have been possible." I signaled for Heidi and Dave to join David and I in the front of the room. The room eyed her, and I could hear whispers as she made her way forward. My emotions were high. My eyes had already started to water. Once they arrived, the four of us embraced just as warmly as we had earlier. Heidi immediately eyed Doc; she was finally within arm's reach of the person she'd nurtured for nine months.

I reached for Doc and held him upright in my arms.

"Everyone, this is Heidi. She is the person who selflessly gave me one of life's greatest blessings, this little guy right here," I said. The crowd applauded and was on their feet. Someone leaned in to hand me a tissue. The tears were so heavy I could hardly see.

"Heidi and Dave, I would like to openly thank you for what you did for us. I look at how much our lives have changed, and it's all because of you. The emptiness of my arms is now visibly full, and the longing I carried to raise a child is a reality. I know that there is no way that I can ever repay you for your kindness, but please know how much I love and appreciate you. I hope you realize that your sacrifice was not in vain."

With that, I extended my arms and placed Doc into hers. There wasn't a dry eye in the room, and the applause was deafening. As he lay in her arms, her smile was wide, looking intently into his eyes. I thought I would be somewhat threatened or maybe even jealous, but all I felt was pure, unadulterated joy. She deserved a moment with her surro-baby, and I wanted her to have it.

The rest of the event went off without a hitch—games, fun, family, and friends doting on Heidi, hugging and thanking her. I also took a moment to thank all my girls for making this day so special.

"Heidi, you will always be in my prayers," said my mom. The entire afternoon was on such a high note, I hated to see it end.

The next day was Doc's baby dedication. It was the final but most important event of the weekend. David and I stood alongside his four godparents. We, along with the church, took vows to care for and love David Joshua. Our pastor, who had married David and I previously, was overjoyed that we'd come this far.

After church, we did the only thing left to do. We all convened at our home and ate a feast fit for a king. The house was packed, the laughs were loud, and the love was genuine, but I knew the next day would bring more tears. Saying goodbye is always hard. That morning I was in a somber mood—the time had finally come to say goodbye to my family and friends. It was hard, especially saying goodbye to my mom. God willing, we'd have many more days to enjoy one another.

I could hear the sound of the garage door opening; David had returned home. My dad had a late flight, and David dropped him off at the airport. My mom was right about putting cereal in the baby's bottle; Doc was fast asleep. My in-laws chose to stay with us for a few additional days, but they'd turned in as well. I'm sure the long weekend had taken a toll on them. It took a toll on all of us. David walked in the door.

"Hey, you must be really tired," he said.

"What?" I asked as he pulled me back to the present.

"Put your seat in the upright position," he said. I had been asleep the entire flight, and we were already preparing to land in New York.

CHAPTER 35

# NEW YORK, NEW YORK

The first day in the city we met up with family, paid our respects at Ground Zero, and took the subway to Canal Street. The text messages were coming in fast and furious as guests arrived in town. That evening, David and I chose to turn in early, as we needed to rest up for all the excitement tomorrow.

I woke up that morning feeling refreshed. The August weather was beautiful, with not a cloud in the sky. The party wasn't until seven o'clock. The biggest shock was that I even wanted a party at all. I've never been one for a lot of fanfare and hoopla; I don't like attention. Well, maybe a little. I had friends who celebrated the entire birthday week, some even months, and I say more power to them. If you don't celebrate you, nobody else will.

The first order of the day was to call Doc.

"David, I'm calling Doc. Would you like to talk to him?" I called into the bathroom.

"Yeah, I'll be right out," he yelled. The phone rang only once before Miss Loretta answered.

"Good morning," I heard her gentle voice say.

"Good morning, Miss Loretta."

"So, today is the big day, right?" she asked.

"Yes, we'll be home tomorrow," I answered.

"Well, let me put him on the phone."

"Hi, Mama," I heard my sweet boy say.

"Hello, sweetie. I miss you," I sighed.

"Miss you," he repeated. David got in on the fun. The calls with Doc were usually brief; there was always a cartoon or a stuffed animal that was more interesting than us.

After the call, I spent hours lounging while David stayed busy on the phone answering questions about the party. My siblings made most of the arrangements. They knew what I liked, and when in doubt, they asked. The plan was for me to board the yacht at one destination with the hosts, and then pick up the guests in another location. It would allow me time to get dressed, then hide out before I made my grand entrance.

"Honey, are you all packed?" asked David. Where did the time go? It was time for us to make our way over to New York Harbor. Once we arrived, I stood in awe of the beauty of these large vessels.

"Hey, girl!" I heard someone scream. I turned around, and there were two of my sisters, Asjah and Aubrey.

"Heeeeyyyyy!" I screamed back. They looked beautiful all decked out in their finest white attire. They'd been hands-on with everything; I couldn't thank them enough.

The interior of the yacht was spectacular.

"So, this is how the other half lives," I said. We all laughed. The huge bar and high-top tables gave it a nice lounge feeling. I found my way to the private dressing room. I chose not to wear white. I wanted to stand out. Instead, I wore a beautiful silver fitted dress, ending just above my knees. The silver jewelry and blinged-out sandals pulled the look together.

"Hey, put this on," said Asjah. She draped a beautiful purple-and-silver sash across my chest. I looked like I was in a pageant, and I loved it.

Once I came out of the room, I noticed that the already spectacular room was transformed into a dedication to me. A huge banner with my picture on it, miniature wine bottles with my name spelled out, and beautiful pink-and-green favors decorated the space. The DJ was already set up and ready to get the party started. My sisters had outdone themselves.

The captain alerted us that it was time to pick up the guests on the other side of the harbor. As they boarded, I was sure to stay in my secluded dressing room. I could hear the music and constant chatter. I could only imagine the mood on the other side of the door. There was a knock, but before opening the door I had to wait for the visitor to announce themselves.

"It's Eden and Courtney," the visitors said. My two other sisters walked into the dressing room, looking amazing in their white attire.

"We had everyone moved to the lower level. It's time for you to make your entrance," Eden said. David planned to make an entrance, then stand at the foot of the steps waiting for me as I confidently made my way down the stairs. My four nephews were waiting for me just outside the door. It was hard to believe that I'd babysat for these grown men. They each wore a white suit and dark shades. The four of them flanked me, two in front and the other two in back.

There was only one song that I wanted to hear during my entrance. With the music of Kelly Rowland as my backdrop, I high-stepped it down the stairs. No one believed that at fifty I could bump like this, but I certainly proved them wrong.

My friends were ecstatic. The last time I'd seen some of them was my baby shower. The moment was electric. There were cheers, screaming, and the beautiful sound of my sorority call. That night I felt like a queen.

As we passed the Statue of Liberty, a group of us stood along the bow and sang "The Star-Spangled Banner." What a wonderful time we had.

At the end of the night, I thanked everyone for coming, but most of all, I thanked the one person who made it all happen—the love of my life, David.

CHAPTER 36

# NOTHING COMPARES TO YOU

As much fun as I had while in New York, my mind focused on what I had at home. I was eager to see Doc, and I knew he was eager to see me.

"Feels good to be back in Atlanta," David said.

"Tell me about it. I'm beat," I added. As we made our way up Georgia 400, I looked over to my handsome husband, and I thought about my beautiful son. It made me smile.

"Let's pick up something to eat before we head home," I said.

"Sounds good. What do you have a taste for?" David asked. I looked around the car quizzically and wondered if this was really my husband. Why would he ask me such a question? He already knew the answer.

"I have an idea. Maybe we could go for Mexican?" I said slyly. Everybody knows I've never met a chimichanga I didn't like.

After picking up our to-go order, we made our way home. We pulled into the driveway where Miss Loretta's car sat in front of the door. I couldn't get into the house fast enough.

"Mama," I heard Doc say. I kneeled and snatched him up into my arms. I held him tight.

"I love you so much," I whispered. I'd gone from a fancy yacht with shrimp and champagne to chicken nuggets and milk, but I wouldn't change a thing.

That night, after Doc fell asleep and I'd put away the last toy, I decided to turn in. David had practically passed out about an hour before. Thoughts of our incredible weekend started to play in my head, but soon took a back seat to thoughts of the good life, my good life now.

I checked the doors, turned on the alarm, and ascended the stairs. I couldn't help but make a stop by Doc's room. He was sleeping peacefully. I gave him a soft peck on the lips before I walked down the hall to my bedroom. David was sleeping peacefully, and I kissed him too.

After a quick shower, I crawled into bed. My body was physically tired, but I couldn't forget to say my prayers.

I can't help but thank you, God, for everything—for family, friends, life, health, wealth, and strength. I'm reminded of where I was and how you brought me out. I'm living in the latter years knowing that they will be better than the former. Getting to this place was hard. At times, my faith wavered and I wanted to give up, but with every battle and every setback, I know it was your setup for something better. Tomorrow is not promised, so today, for all that I am and all that I hope to be, Lord, I say thank you.

# EPILOGUE

*Two Years Later*

The first day of pre-K is always exciting. It was emotional dropping off Doc that morning. He looked so cute in his khaki shorts and light-blue polo shirt. I could hardly believe he was already four years old.

He and his dad would be home any minute, and I was excited to hear about his first day. Suddenly, a cute little boy burst through the door.

"Mommy!" shouted Doc. I knelt so he could run into my arms.

"Hello, Docey-Pooh. How was your day?" I asked.

"We did coloring, and we had to make a picture of our family." Doc dug into his book bag to retrieve his picture.

"See, this is Daddy, and this is you, and this is me," he lovingly said.

"And who is this? One of your little friends at school?" I asked.

He laughed. "Mommy, it's my sister. I want a sister."

. . . Blank Stare.

# About the Author

Kimberly Gowdy's debut work weaves her narrative based on life experience in the world of infertility and surrogacy. Her writing style and attention to detail will leave readers wanting more from this aspiring author. Kimberly is a seasoned insurance executive. She is married and lives in Johns Creek, Georgia.

www.ingramcontent.com/pod-product-compliance
Lightning Source LLC
Chambersburg PA
CBHW060522080526
44586CB00012B/573